About this workbook

This book contains questions to target every topic in Year 5 Maths.

Questions split into three levels of increasing difficulty – Challenge 1, Challenge 2 and Challenge 3 – to aid progress.

'How am I doing?' checks for self-evaluation.

Handy tips included.

Total marks boxes for each topic.

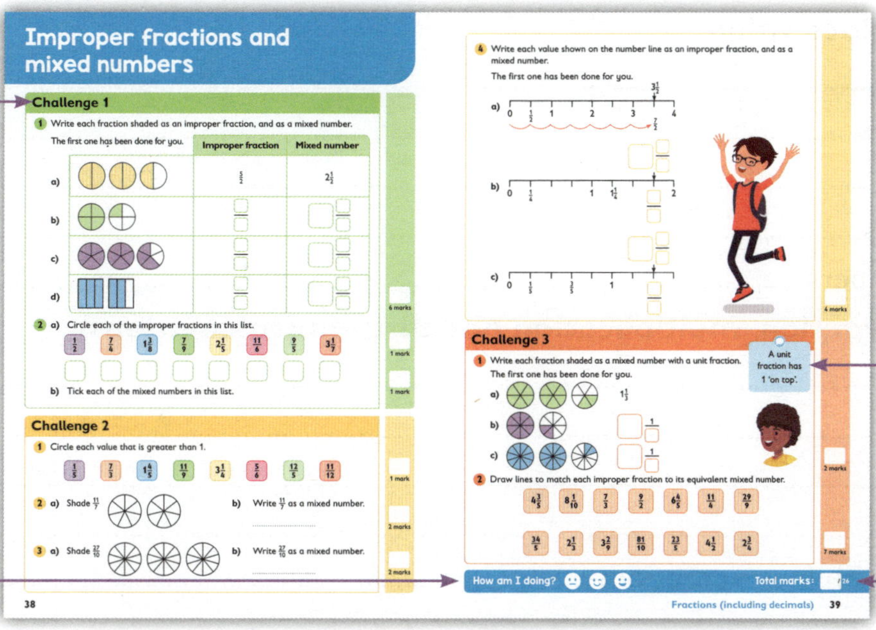

Starter test recaps skills covered in Years 3 and 4.

Four progress tests allow children to test how well they have remembered the information.

QR codes link to online interactive quizzes for extra practice.

Progress test charts to record results and identify which areas need further practice.

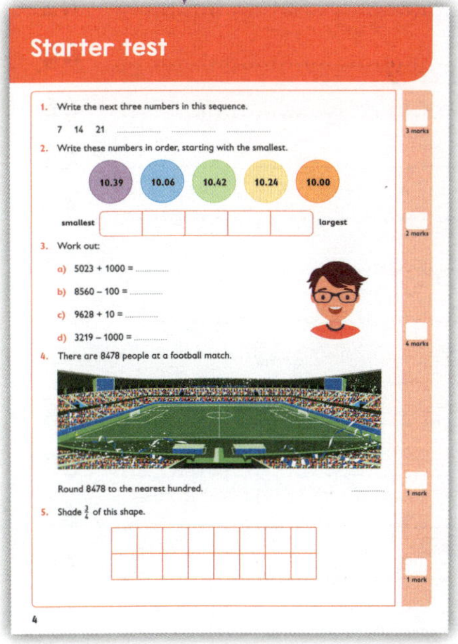

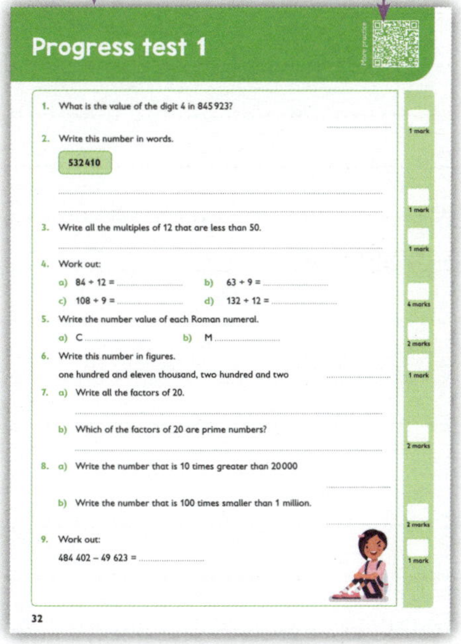

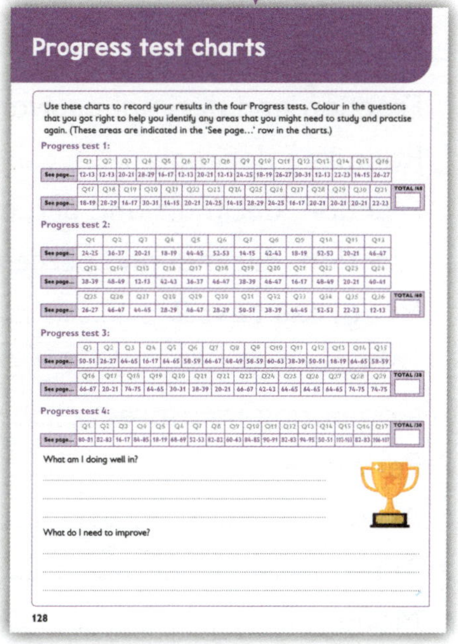

Answers are included at the back of the book.

Author: Katherine Pate

Contents

Starter test	4
Number and place value	
Place value	12
Rounding numbers	14
Roman numerals	16
Negative numbers	18
Properties of numbers	20
Addition, subtraction, multiplication and division (calculations)	
Addition	22
Subtraction	24
Multiplication	26
Division	28
Problem solving with four operations	30
Progress test 1	32
Fractions (including decimals)	
Equivalent fractions	36
Improper fraction and mixed numbers	38
Comparing and ordering fractions	40
Adding and subtracting fractions	42
Multiplying fractions	44
Fraction and decimal equivalents	46
Rounding decimals	48
Fraction, decimals and percentages	50
Fraction, decimal and percentage problems	52
Progress test 2	54
Measures	
Comparing measures	58
Perimeter	60
Area	62
Time	64
Money	66
Volume and capacity	68
Metric and imperial units	70
Scaling problems	72
Problem solving with measures	74
Progress test 3	76

Contents

Geometry – properties of shapes
Types of angle	80
Calculating angles	82
Polygons	84
2-D shapes	86
Properties of rectangles	88
Properties of triangles	90
3-D shapes	92

Geometry – position and direction
Coordinates	94
Translations	96
Reflections	98

Statistics
Tables	100
Timetables	102
Bar charts and pictograms	104
Line graphs	106
Progress test 4	108
Answers	112
Progress test charts	128

ACKNOWLEDGEMENTS

The author and publisher are grateful to the copyright holders for permission to use quoted materials and images.

All illustrations and images are © Shutterstock.com and © HarperCollins*Publishers*

Every effort has been made to trace copyright holders and obtain their permission for the use of copyright material. The author and publisher will gladly receive information enabling them to rectify any error or omission in subsequent editions. All facts are correct at time of going to press.

Without limiting the exclusive rights of any author, contributor or the publisher, any unauthorised use of this publication to train generative artificial intelligence (AI) technologies is expressly prohibited. HarperCollins also exercise their rights under Article 4(3) of the Digital Single Market Directive 2019/790 and expressly reserve this publication from the text and data mining exception.

Published by Collins
An imprint of HarperCollins*Publishers*
1 London Bridge Street
London SE1 9GF

HarperCollins*Publishers*
Macken House, 39/40 Mayor Street Upper,
Dublin 1, D01 C9W8, Ireland

© HarperCollins*Publishers* Limited 2025
ISBN 9780008727871
First published 2025
10 9 8 7 6 5 4 3 2 1

All rights reserved. No part of this publication may be reproduced, stored in a retrieval system, or transmitted, in any form or by any means, electronic, mechanical, photocopying, recording or otherwise, without the prior permission of Collins.

British Library Cataloguing in Publication Data.

A CIP record of this book is available from the British Library.

Publisher: Fiona McGlade
Author: Katherine Pate
Contributor: Ali Simpson
Project manager and editorial: Chantal Addy
Cover design: Sarah Duxbury
Inside concept design: Ian Wrigley
Text design and layout: Rose & Thorn Creative Services Ltd
Artwork: Shutterstock and Collins
Production: Bethany Brohm
Printed in India by Multivista Global Pvt.Ltd.

MIX
Paper | Supporting responsible forestry
FSC™ C007454

Starter test

1. Write the next three numbers in this sequence.

   7   14   21   ....   **3 marks**

2. Write these numbers in order, starting with the smallest.

   smallest ☐☐☐☐☐ largest   **2 marks**

3. Work out:

   a) 5023 + 1000 = ...

   b) 8560 − 100 = ...

   c) 9628 + 10 = ...

   d) 3219 − 1000 = ...   **4 marks**

4. There are **8478** people at a football match.

   Round 8478 to the nearest hundred.   ....   **1 mark**

5. Shade $\frac{3}{4}$ of this shape.

   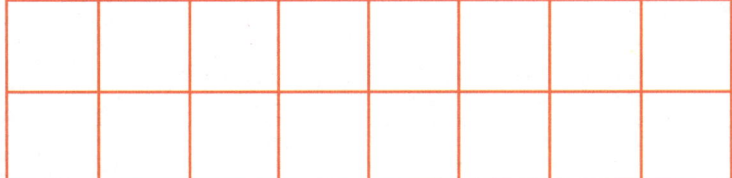

   1 mark

6. Connor has £20. He buys:

a water bottle for £6.25

a lunch box for £8.99

How much money does Connor have left?

£...................

1 mark

7. This rectangle is drawn on a 1 cm² grid.

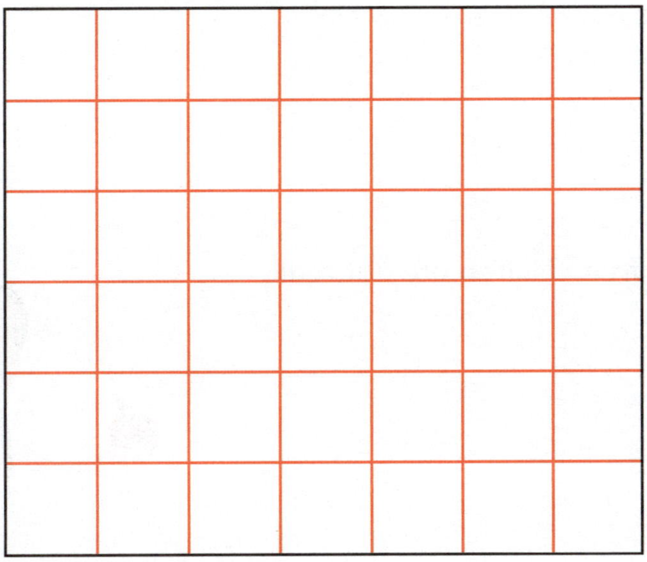

Work out the area of this rectangle. ....cm²

1 mark

8. Write these Roman numerals in numbers.

a) XV ....

b) XXXIX ....

c) XC ....

d) LIV ....

4 marks

9. a) Write this number in words.

> 2468

....

b) Write this number in figures.

one thousand and seventeen ....

2 marks

Starter test 5

10. Work out the perimeter of this square.

6 cm

..............cm

11. Circle the largest number in each pair.

a) 10 000 or 7999

b) 27 300 or 28 900

c) 19 317 or 19 371

d) 94 500 or 100 000

12. The bar chart shows the fruit children ate at break.

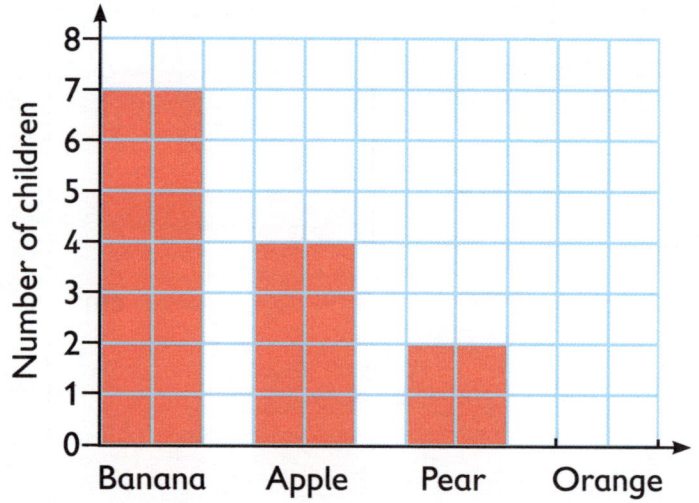

a) 6 children ate an orange.

Draw a bar on the bar chart to show this.

b) How many children ate fruit at break?

....

c) How many more children ate a banana than ate a pear?

....

13. Here is a coordinate grid.

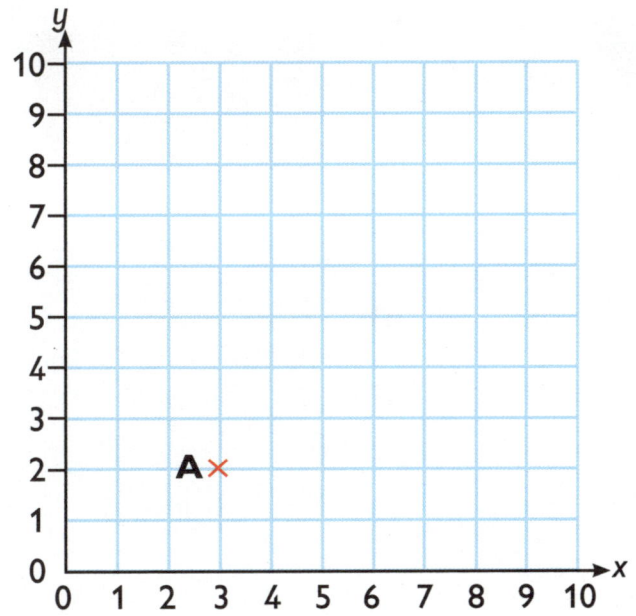

a) Write the coordinates of point A. (........, ...)

b) Plot point B at (7, 2)

Join point A to point B with a straight line.

c) Plot two more points and join them to A and B to make a square.

3 marks

14. Draw lines to match each fraction to a decimal.

| $\frac{7}{10}$ | $\frac{1}{2}$ | $\frac{1}{4}$ | $\frac{3}{100}$ | $\frac{3}{4}$ |

| 0.75 | 0.03 | 0.7 | 0.25 | 0.5 |

2 marks

15. How many metres are there in 1 kilometre? ....m

1 mark

16. A film starts at 6.15 pm.

The film is 90 minutes long.

What time does the film finish? ....pm

1 mark

Starter test 7

17. Write the names of these quadrilaterals.

a)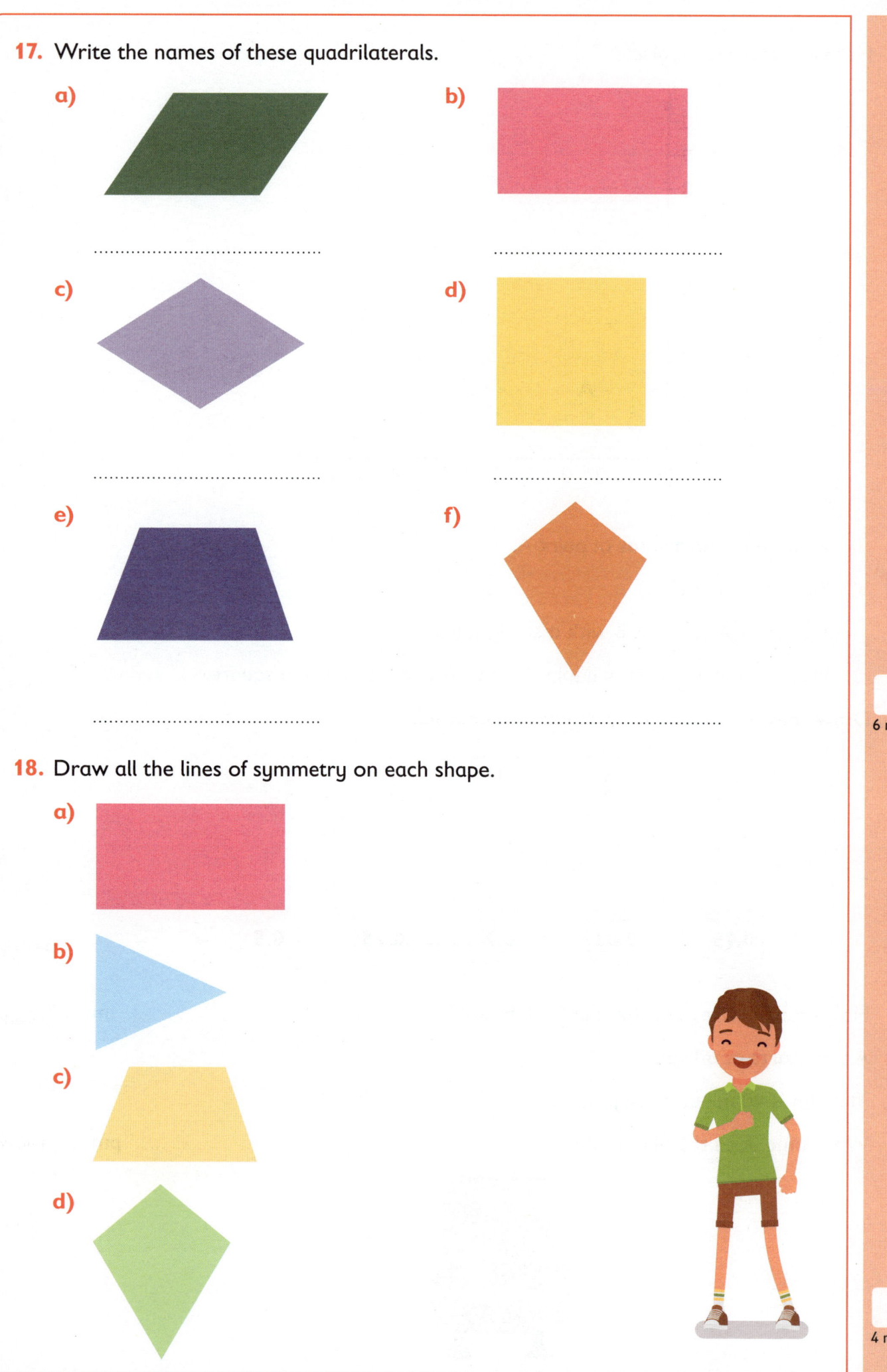

....

b)

....

c)

....

d)

....

e)

....

f)

....

6 marks

18. Draw all the lines of symmetry on each shape.

a)

b)

c)

d)

4 marks

19. Here are some angles.

a) 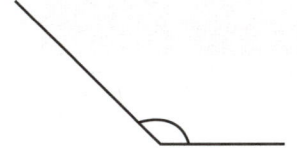　　b) 　　c)

d) 　　e) 　　f)

Write A on the acute angles.

Write O on the obtuse angles.

Write R on the right angles.

6 marks

20. Shade squares in the bottom half of this diagram to make it symmetrical about the line of symmetry.

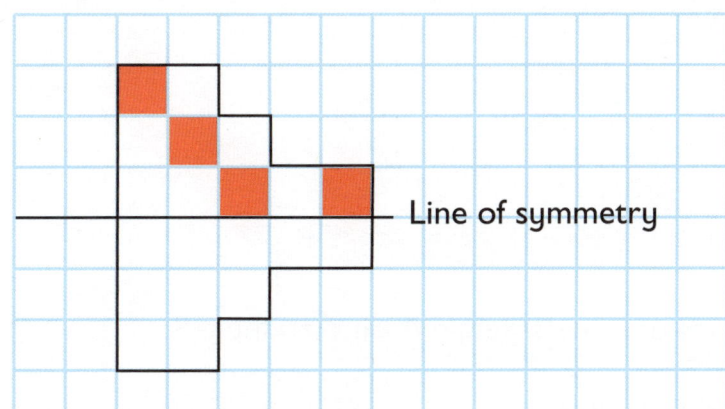

1 mark

21. This clock shows a time in the afternoon.

a) Write this time as a pm time. .... pm

b) Write this time using the 24-hour clock. ....

2 marks

22. Write in the missing numbers.

a) 1 hour = ... minutes

b) 1 week = ... days

c) 365 days = ... year

d) 24 hours = ... day

e) 1 minute = ... seconds

f) March has .... days.

23. Here are two triangles on a squared grid.

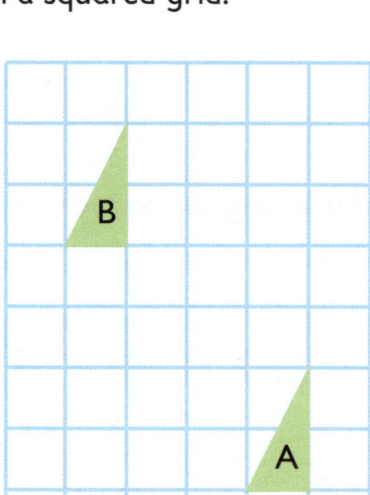

Complete the instructions to move triangle A onto triangle B.

.... squares left and 4 squares ....

24. Write the numbers in the boxes on this number line.

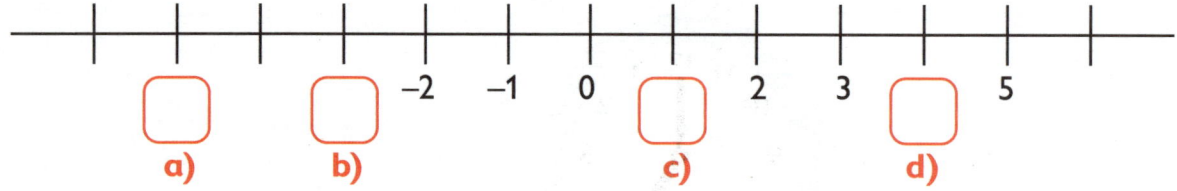

a)   b)   c)   d)

25. Work out:

a) 3270 + 495 = ...

b) 1200 − 310 = ...

2 marks

26. Work out:

a) 8 × 6 = ...

b) 72 ÷ 9 = ...

c) 108 ÷ 12 = ...

d) 11 × 11 = ...

4 marks

27. Work out:

    427
×   3
....

....

1 mark

28. Write the next three numbers in this sequence.

5.26   5.24   5.22   ....

3 marks

29. Work out:

a) $\frac{2}{6} + \frac{3}{6}$ = ...

b) $\frac{5}{9} - \frac{1}{9}$ = ...

c) $1 - \frac{1}{7}$ = ...

d) $1 - \frac{3}{5}$ = ...

4 marks

30. Work out:

a) $\frac{1}{5}$ of 30 = ...

b) $\frac{7}{10}$ of 20 = ...

2 marks

How am I doing?   Total marks: ☐ /81

Starter test   **11**

Place value

Challenge 1

1. Write the missing numbers in this sequence.

   1840   2840   ....

   3 marks

2. a) Write this number in words.

   14 287

   ....

   ....

   1 mark

   b) Write this number in figures.

   twenty thousand ....

   1 mark

   c) Write this number in figures.

   one million ....

   1 mark

3. Write these numbers in order, starting with the smallest.

   | 70 047 | 470 000 | 407 020 | 74 740 | 407 006 |

   smallest [ ][ ][ ][ ][ ] largest

   2 marks

Challenge 2

1. Write each number in figures.

   a) two hundred and three thousand, six hundred and one   ....

   b) six hundred thousand, five hundred and thirty   ....

   2 marks

2. Here are some children's scores in a computer game.

   | Petra | 754 109 | Sammy | 759 184 | Lily | 754 119 |
   | Anisa | 760 367 | Miguel | 759 185 | Robbie | 759 439 |

   Jack writes these scores in order, starting with the largest.

   Whose score is 5th in Jack's list?   ....

   1 mark

3 a) Circle the numbers that have 4 as the hundreds digit.

483 296   1 392 482   37 476   284 395   583 406

☐ ☐ ☐ ☐ ☐

b) Tick (✓) the numbers that have 3 as the thousands digit.

5 marks

Challenge 3

1 Start with this number: 79 496

Write the number that is:

a) 1 more ....   b) 10 more ....

c) 100 more ....   d) 1000 more ....

e) 10 000 more ....   f) 100 000 more ....

6 marks

2 Write the missing numbers in this table.

Number	100 000 more than the number
563 000	
970 251	
	1 136 050
	2 million

4 marks

3 Work out:

a) 489 000 ÷ 10 = ...

b) 489 000 ÷ 1000 = ...

c) 489 000 ÷ 100 = ...

3 marks

4 Write each number in figures.

a) 12 tens ....   b) 12 hundreds ....

c) 12 thousands ....   d) 12 hundred thousands ....

4 marks

5 What is 11 thousands plus 11 hundreds? ....

1 mark

How am I doing?   Total marks: ☐ / 34

Rounding numbers

Challenge 1

1 Round these numbers to the nearest thousand.

a) 6593 .... b) 27 380 ....

c) 18 730 .... d) 329 120 ....

e) 742 503 .... f) 38 294 ....

6 marks

2 Here are some numbers:

| 9842 | 9926 | 10 500 | 9860 | 9835 | 10 312 |

a) Which numbers in the box round to 9840 to the nearest 10?
....

b) Which numbers in the box round to 9900 to the nearest 100?
....

c) Which numbers in the box round to 10 000 to the nearest 1000?
....

6 marks

Challenge 2

1 Round these numbers to the nearest ten thousand.

a) 82 390 .... b) 29 503 ....

c) 193 439 .... d) 293 663 ....

e) 275 589 .... f) 555 537 ....

6 marks

2 Round these numbers to the nearest hundred thousand.

a) 283 478 .... b) 329 894 ....

c) 107 038 .... d) 482 002 ....

e) 945 439 .... f) 675 000 ....

6 marks

14

3 Marie has 73 672 online followers.

Write the number of followers to the nearest thousand. .... 1 mark

4 There are 184 820 ants in a colony.

How many ants are there to the nearest ten thousand?

.... 1 mark

Challenge 3

1 Round 950 000 to the nearest hundred thousand. .... 1 mark

2 a) What is the largest number that rounds to 30 000 to the nearest 10 000?

....

b) What is the smallest number that rounds to 30 000 to the nearest 10 000?

.... 2 marks

3 Round each number in the calculation to the nearest 1000 to estimate the answer to the calculation.

The first one has been done for you.

a) 27 145 ÷ 2900   Estimate: 27 000 ÷ 3000 = 9

b) 8420 ÷ 1800   Estimate: ....

c) 84 000 ÷ 19 750   Estimate: ....

2 marks

4 Round each number so it only has one non-zero digit.

The first one has been done for you:

a) 2931   3000   b) 412   ....

c) 35   ....   d) 54 000   ....

e) 327 000   ....   f) 496 102   ....

5 marks

5 a) Round each number so it only has one non-zero digit.

3784   ....   61 257   ....

2 marks

b) Use your rounded numbers to estimate the answer to this calculation.

3784 + 61 257   Estimate: ....

1 mark

How am I doing?   Total marks: ...... /39

Roman numerals

Challenge 1

1. Write the number value of each Roman numeral.

   a) V ....   b) I ....   c) X ....

   d) C ....   e) L ....

   5 marks

2. The contents list in a book starts on page I and ends on page XII.

   How many pages long is the contents list? ....

   1 mark

3. Write these Roman numerals in order, starting with the smallest.

   | LXXIV | XXVII | XC | XLIX | XXXIII |

   smallest [ ][ ][ ][ ][ ] largest

   2 marks

4. a) Write down the largest number you can make using each of these Roman numerals once.

   | L | I | V | X |

   ....

   b) Write down the smallest number you can make using each of these Roman numerals once.

   | C | I | V | X |

   ....

   2 marks

Challenge 2

1. Write the number value of each Roman numeral.

   a) D ....   b) M ....

   2 marks

2. King Ethelbert died in DCVI.

   Write this year in ordinary numbers. ....

   1 mark

16

3 The Battle of Leicester was in MDCXLV.

Write this year in ordinary numbers. .... 1 mark

4 King Henry VIII married Anne Boleyn in MDXXXIII.

Write this year in ordinary numbers. .... 1 mark

Challenge 3

1 Work out these calculations and write your answers in ordinary numbers.

   a) IV + XX = ...

   b) V × VI = ...

   c) XXIII + VIII = ...

   d) L + XXV = ...

   e) CLIX + XXVI = ...

   f) CXC + XL = ...

   g) DCVII − CCII = ...

   h) M ÷ X = ...

8 marks

2 The first TV show in the UK was in MCMXXXVI.

Write this year in ordinary numbers. .... 1 mark

3 Write the missing numbers in this sequence.

....   CLX   CLXXX   ....

3 marks

4 The Curiosity space craft landed on Mars in MMXII.

Write this year in ordinary numbers.

....

1 mark

How am I doing?   Total marks: ☐ /28

Number and place value   17

Negative numbers

Challenge 1

1 Here is a number line.

Write in the missing numbers in the boxes.

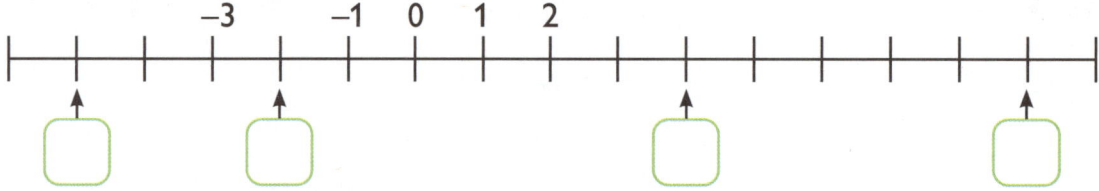

4 marks

2 This thermometer shows a temperature of 3°C.

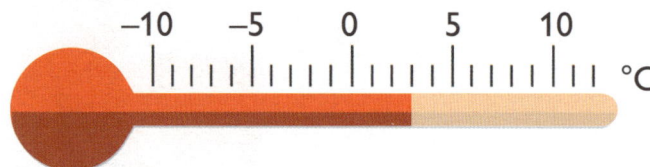

a) The temperature falls by 3 degrees.

What is the new temperature? ....°C

b) What temperature is 4 degrees higher than 3°C? ....°C

c) What temperature is 5 degrees lower than 3°C? ....°C

3 marks

3 Circle the colder temperature in each pair.

a) 6°C   8°C   b) –4°C   0°C

c) –5°C   –2°C   d) –14°C   –18°C

4 marks

Challenge 2

1 Write these temperatures in order, starting with the lowest.

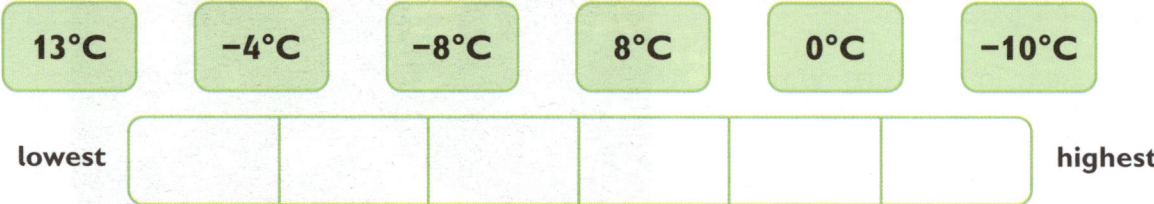

2 marks

2 Write these temperatures in order, starting with the highest.

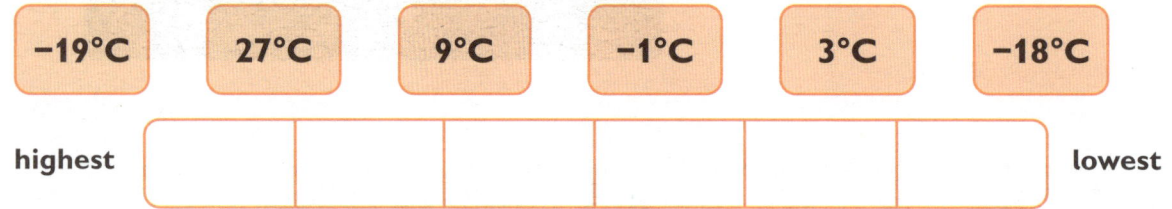

2 marks

3 The temperature is 5°C and it falls by 8°C.

What is the new temperature? ....°C 1 mark

4 The temperature is −6°C and it rises by 10°C.

What is the new temperature? ....°C 1 mark

5 The temperature is −9°C and it rises by 4°C.

What is the new temperature? ....°C 1 mark

Challenge 3

1 At 9 am the temperature is −3°C. The temperature rises 2 degrees every hour.

What is the temperature at 1 pm? ....°C 1 mark

2 The temperature starts at −1°C. It rises by 7 degrees and then falls 3 degrees.

What is the final temperature? ....°C 1 mark

3 Here are the buttons in a lift.

a) Ruby gets in the lift on the 6th floor.

She wants to go down to the ground floor.

Which button should she press?

....

b) Tom gets in the lift in the underground car park, at level −2.

He presses the button for the 3rd floor.

How many floors does he go up?

....

c) Ali gets in the lift on the 2nd floor.
The lift goes down 3 floors and then up 5 floors.

Which floor is Ali on now? .... 3 marks

4 Here are the temperatures in two cities one day in January.

Helsinki −4°C   Reykjavik −9°C

Helsinki is warmer than Reykjavik.

How many degrees warmer? .... 1 mark

How am I doing?   Total marks: ____ /24

Number and place value   19

Properties of numbers

Challenge 1

1. Write the first four multiples of 9.

   .... *1 mark*

2. Write all the factors of 8.

   .... *1 mark*

3. Work out:

   a) $5^2 = 5 \times 5 = $ ....
   b) $10^2 = $ ....
   c) $1^2 = $ ....
   d) $6^2 = $ ....

   4 marks

4. Circle all the prime numbers in this list.

   1   2   3   5   7   9   11

   2 marks

Challenge 2

1. Work out:

   a) $1^3 = 1 \times 1 \times 1 = $ ....
   b) $2^3 = $ ....
   c) $3^3 = $ ....
   d) $10^3 = $ ....

   4 marks

2. Write four multiples of 7 that are odd numbers less than 100.

   .... *2 marks*

3. What are the odd factors of 12?

   .... *1 mark*

4. What are the common factors of 28 and 16?

   .... *2 marks*

5. Circle all the square numbers in this grid.

1	2	3	4	5	6	7	8	9	10
11	12	13	14	15	16	17	18	19	20

   2 marks

6. Circle all the prime numbers in this grid

11	12	13	14	15	16	17	18	19	20
21	22	23	24	25	26	27	28	29	30

   2 marks

20

7 Write the missing numbers in these calculations.

a) ☐² = 49

b) ☐² = 81

c) ☐³ = 64 = ☐²

4 marks

Challenge 3

1 Write the missing number in this sequence.

1   4   9   25   36

1 mark

2 a) What is the smallest 2-digit prime number? ....

b) What is the largest 2-digit prime number? ....

2 marks

3 Which two square numbers less than 20 add together make another square number?

....

1 mark

4 Work out:

a) $6^2 + 8^2$ = ...   b) $5^2 - 4^2$ = ...

c) $8^2 \div 2^2$ = ...   d) $10^2 \times 3^2$ = ...

4 marks

5 Work out:

a) $3^3 \times 2$ = ...   b) $2^3 + 4^2$ = ...

c) $5^3 - 9^2$ = ...   d) $4^3 + 10^3$ = ...

4 marks

6 a) Write down the first five cube numbers:

....

2 marks

b) Which two cube numbers are also square numbers? ....

2 marks

7 In these addition pyramids, add two numbers to get the number in the space above. Complete both pyramids.

a)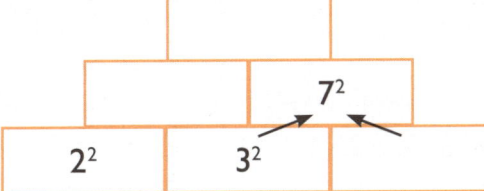

b)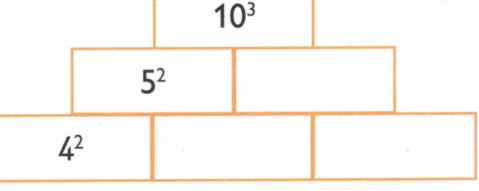

6 marks

How am I doing?   Total marks: ☐ /47

Number and place value   21

Addition

Challenge 1

1 Work out mentally:

a) 10 000 + 4500 = ...

b) 380 000 + 20 000 = ...

c) 52 300 + 1200 = ...

d) 102 460 + 1500 = ...

4 marks

2 Work out:

a)   4531
  + 2457
  ....

  ....

b)   37602
  + 21359
  ....

  ....

c)   98312
  + 2946
  ....

  ....

d)   537999
  + 41370
  ....

  ....

4 marks

3 In these addition pyramids, add two numbers to get the number in the space above.

Complete both the pyramids.

a)

570	350	420

With 570 + 350 = in middle row.

b)

9760	280	3300

6 marks

Challenge 2

1 Work out:

a) 27 650 + 8200 = ...

b) 490 320 + 25 275 = ...

c) 68 400 + 390 500 = ...

d) 125 670 + 9815 = ...

4 marks

22

2. a) Circle two numbers that add to 2000.

   1350   750   950   1150   650   800

   b) Circle two numbers that add to 100 000.

   45 325   65 675   54 675   35 325   64 775

   2 marks

3. An airport records the number of passengers flying each day one weekend.

Saturday	327 017
Sunday	407 361

   How many passengers were there over the whole weekend?

   ....

   1 mark

4. Use these digits once each in this addition calculation to make the largest total possible.

   2   3   4   5   6   7   8   9

   ☐☐☐☐ + ☐☐☐☐ = ☐☐☐☐☐

   2 marks

Challenge 3

1. Four athletes do a charity bike ride.

   The table shows the number of metres they cycled each day.

Athlete	Monday	Tuesday	Wednesday	Thursday	Friday
Riya	23 493	10 293	22 371	9394	42 092
Max	18 273	21 384	54 109	23 384	55 092
Hannah	10 273	53 235	33 482	18 492	56 099
Ashok	29 302	47 038	39 272	8092	9309

   a) Which athlete cycled the greatest distance in total?   ....

   b) Which day did the four athletes cover the greatest total distance?

   ....

   2 marks

How am I doing?   Total marks: ☐ /25

Addition, subtraction, multiplication and division (calculations)

Subtraction

Challenge 1

1. Work out mentally:

   a) 7850 − 240 = ...   b) 25 000 − 8000 = ...

   c) 40 700 − 10 250 = ...   d) 320 400 − 19 300 = ...

2. Work out:

   a)   8543   b)   59416   c)   95261   d)   346000

   − 2412   − 15208   − 2346   −119350

4 marks

4 marks

Challenge 2

1. Work out:

   a)   20000   b)   600000

     − 4715   − 25375

2 marks

2. Work out:

   a) 29 374 − 8349 = ...   b) 39 023 − 9403 = ...

   c) 65 028 − 9482 = ...   d) 94 859 − 28 458 = ...

4 marks

3. Chapton football ground has seats for home fans and away fans.

   There are 40 570 seats in total.

   8029 seats are for away fans.

   How many seats are for the home fans? ....

1 mark

24

4 In these addition pyramids, add two numbers to get the number in the space above. Complete both the pyramids.

a)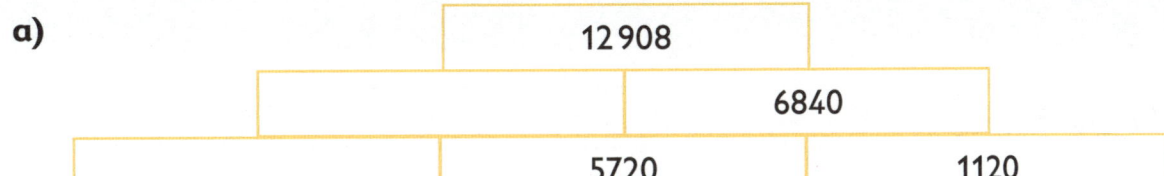

b)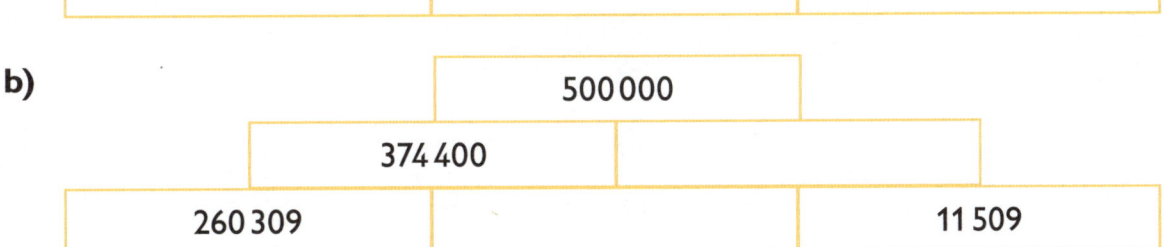

5 Find the missing numbers.

a) 48 923 − ☐ = 36 138   b) ☐ − 24 812 = 32 168

c) 99 842 − ☐ = 15 627   d) ☐ − 74 206 = 50 481

6 An airport records the number of passengers flying each day one weekend.

| Saturday | 327 017 |
| Sunday | 407 361 |

How many more passengers were there on Sunday than on Saturday?

....

Challenge 3

1 Work out the missing numbers in these calculations.

a) 14 457 + ☐ = 19 880   b) 74 404 + ☐ = 83 393

c) 84 330 + ☐ = 101 352   d) 105 576 + ☐ = 129 417

2 In one year, Alex earned £32 400. In that year he spent:

£9600 on rent   £3640 on food   £4995 on a car

How much money did he have left?

....

How am I doing?   Total marks: ☐ /29

Addition, subtraction, multiplication and division (calculations)

Multiplication

Challenge 1

1 Work out:

a) 5 × 12 = ... b) 8 × 9 = ...

c) 7 × 6 = ... d) 11 × 12 = ...

e) 9 × 7 = ... f) 6 × 8 = ...

6 marks

2 Work out mentally:

a) 2970 × 10 = ... b) 5180 × 100 = ...

c) 3507 × 100 = ... d) 1000 × 472 = ...

e) 46 215 × 10 = ... f) 10 000 × 25 = ...

6 marks

3 Work out:

a) 54
  × 7
  ....

  ....

b) 312
  × 4
  ....

  ....

c) 86
  × 6
  ....

  ....

d) 527
  × 8
  ....

  ....

4 marks

Challenge 2

1 Work out:

a) $2^2 × 3^2$ = ... b) $8^2 × 5^2$ = ...

c) $3^3 × 2^3$ = ... d) $10^3 × 6^2$ = ...

4 marks

2. Work out:

a) 342 × 21

b) 135 × 34

c) 3582 × 18

d) 4163 × 51

4 marks

3. There are 365 days in a year.

There are 24 hours in a day.

Work out the number of hours in a year.

....

1 mark

Challenge 3

1. The distance from Edinburgh to Malaga is 2144 km.
An aeroplane flies from Edinburgh to Malaga and back, five days a week.

How far does the aeroplane fly in total in one week?

....

1 mark

2. Work out mentally:

a) 142 × 20 = ...

b) 1213 × 300 = ...

c) 424 × 2000 = ...

d) 56 × 20 000 = ...

4 marks

3. Write the first five prime numbers in the empty boxes.

Then work out the multiplication.

☐ × ☐ × ☐ × ☐ × ☐ = ☐

2 marks

4. This box contains 42 packets of biscuits.   There are 18 biscuits in one packet.

How many biscuits are there in 12 of these boxes?

....

1 mark

How am I doing?   Total marks: ☐ /33

Addition, subtraction, multiplication and division (calculations)

Division

Challenge 1

1 Work out:

a) 72 ÷ 12 = ... b) 54 ÷ 9 = ...

c) 96 ÷ 8 = ... d) 121 ÷ 11 = ...

e) 56 ÷ 7 = ... f) 45 ÷ 9 = ...

6 marks

2 Work out mentally:

a) 2560 ÷ 10 = ... b) 95 000 ÷ 100 = ...

c) 253 100 ÷ 100 = ... d) 500 000 ÷ 1000 = ...

e) 342 000 ÷ 100 = ... f) 1 000 000 ÷ 1000 = ...

6 marks

3 Work out:

a) 3)126 b) 7)252

c) 6)7338 d) 8)1000

4 marks

4 One brick is 9 cm long.
Liam is building a wall 162 cm long with these bricks.

How many of these bricks does he need?

....

1 mark

Challenge 2

1 Work out:

a) 492 ÷ 4 = ... b) 2688 ÷ 7 = ...

c) 4686 ÷ 6 = ... d) 1575 ÷ 3 = ...

4 marks

2) An egg box holds six eggs.

A farmer has 350 eggs.

a) How many egg boxes can he fill with 350 eggs?

....

b) How many eggs are left over?

.... 2 marks

3) A restaurant needs enough tables for 123 people.

One table has room for 8 people.

How many tables does the restaurant need?

.... 1 mark

4) Jonny has five bags of marbles.

Each bag contains 24 marbles.

Jonny shares all the marbles equally with between himself and 3 friends.

How many marbles does each person get?

.... 1 mark

Challenge 3

1) Work out these divisions and state the remainder each time.

a) 6151 ÷ 4 = ...   b) 3000 ÷ 9 = ...

c) 5000 ÷ 12 = ...   d) 2720 ÷ 11 = ...

4 marks

2) Write the missing numbers in the boxes to make each calculation correct.

a) 8 × ☐ = 5456   b) 11 × ☐ = 5093

2 marks

3) a) Is 9 a factor of 1062?

Explain how you know.

....

b) Is 1850 a multiple of 12?

Explain how you know.

....

2 marks

How am I doing?   Total marks: ☐ / 33

Addition, subtraction, multiplication and division (calculations)   29

Problem solving with four operations

Challenge 1

1. The table shows some information about the number of pupils in Oak Farm School.

Year group	Number of pupils
3	233
4	182
5	252
6	
Total	842

How many pupils are in Year 6?

.... 1 mark

2. There are 729 people on a train to Southampton.

At the first stop, 68 people get off the train and 39 people get on the train.

How many people are on the train after the first stop?

.... 1 mark

3. A multi-storey car park has 620 spaces.

There are the same number of spaces on each level.

There are five levels.

How many spaces are there on each level?

.... 1 mark

4. Jumpers cost £16 each.

T-shirts cost £9 each.

Work out the total cost of 24 jumpers and 15 T-shirts.

.... 1 mark

Challenge 2

1. David cycles for 45 minutes, three times in every week.

    How long will he cycle for in:

    a) 2 weeks .... hours .... minutes

    b) 6 weeks .... hours .... minutes

    2 marks

2. Here is a recipe to make two smoothies:

    1 banana
    100 g strawberries
    4 scoops ice cream
    500 ml milk

    Write in the amounts to make five smoothies.

    .... bananas

    .... strawberries

    .... scoops ice cream

    .... ml milk

    4 marks

3. Four people go out for meal. Between them they eat:

    4 pizzas
    3 salads
    1 portion of chips
    2 ice creams
    1 brownie

    They share the total cost between them equally.

    How much does each person pay?

    Price list
    Pizza £8
    Salad £4
    Chips £3
    Ice cream £2
    Brownie £1

    £...............

    1 mark

Challenge 3

1. Lissa and Niall have 187 football cards in total.

    Lissa has 23 more cards than Niall.

    How many cards do they each have?

    Niall ....   Lissa ....

    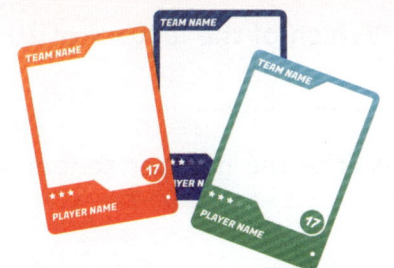

    2 marks

2. Make the scales balance by writing in the correct numbers.

    a) 14 × 32   7 × ....

    b) 142 × 78   .... × 39

    2 marks

How am I doing?   Total marks: ☐ /15

Addition, subtraction, multiplication and division (calculations)   31

Progress test 1

1. What is the value of the digit 4 in 845 923?

   .... 1 mark

2. Write this number in words.

   532 410

   ....
   ....
   1 mark

3. Write all the multiples of 12 that are less than 50.

   ....
   1 mark

4. Work out:

   a) 84 ÷ 12 = ... b) 63 ÷ 9 = ...

   c) 108 ÷ 9 = ... d) 132 ÷ 12 = ...

   4 marks

5. Write the number value of each Roman numeral.

   a) C .... b) M ....

   2 marks

6. Write this number in figures.

   one hundred and eleven thousand, two hundred and two   ....

   1 mark

7. a) Write all the factors of 20.

   ....

   b) Which of the factors of 20 are prime numbers?

   ....

   2 marks

8. a) Write the number that is 10 times greater than 20 000

   ....

   b) Write the number that is 100 times smaller than 1 million.

   ....

   2 marks

9. Work out:

   484 402 − 49 623 = ...

   1 mark

10. Write these temperatures in order, starting with the coldest.

3°C   −2°C   −6°C   5°C   0°C   −4°C

coldest [ ] [ ] [ ] [ ] [ ] [ ] warmest

11. Work out:

$$\begin{array}{r} 426 \\ \times\ \ 35 \\ \hline \end{array}$$

12. A factory has 15 246 pies at the start of the day.

During the day the factory makes 72 000 more pies.

58 320 pies are taken away from the factory to be sold in shops.

How many pies are left in the factory at the end of the day?

13. Write the missing numbers in this table.

1000 less than the number	Number	100 000 more than the number
	27 000	
	249 000	
		1 million

14. There were 48 230 train passengers on Saturday.

On Sunday there were 15 000 fewer train passengers.

How many passengers were there over the whole weekend?

15. Round 35 249 to the nearest 100

Progress test 1   33

16. Miriam walks 8500 steps every day, for two weeks.

How many steps does she walk in total?

....

17. The temperature is −3°C and it rises by 7°C.

What is the new temperature?

..............................°C

18. Work out:

4140 ÷ 3 = ...

19. Dara was born in the year MMVIII.

Write this year in numbers. ....

20. There are 500 sheets of paper in the printer.

Donna prints 22 documents.

Each document uses 16 sheets of paper.

How many sheets of paper are left in the printer?

....

21. Round 108 252 to the nearest ten thousand

....

22. What are the common factors of 36 and 28?

....

23. Leo is trying to raise £1 million for charity.

So far, he has raised £756 219

How much more does he need to raise?

£..............................

24. a) Round 48 280 to the nearest 1000 ....

b) Round 5507 to the nearest 1000 ....

c) Use your rounded values to estimate the answer to 48 280 + 5507

....

25. Work out:

  a) 36 020 ÷ 10 = ...

  b) 536 000 ÷ 1000 = ...

  c) 999 000 ÷ 100 = ...

26. A blue whale weighs 146 000 kg. A whale shark weighs 29 500 kg.

Which is heavier, and by how much?

....

27. Write the year MCMXXXVI in numbers. ....

28. Add together all the factors of 12.

....

29. Write down all the cube numbers less than 30.

....

30. Work out:

  a) $10^3 + 8^2$ = ...

  b) $9^2 - 4^2$ = ...

31. In 2022, the populations of the four countries in the United Kingdom were:

England	57 106 000
Wales	3 132 000
Scotland	5 448 000
Northern Ireland	1 911 000

Work out the total population of the UK in 2022.

....

How am I doing?

Total marks: ☐ / 48

Progress test 1   35

Equivalent fractions

Challenge 1

1. What fraction of each shape is shaded?

   a) 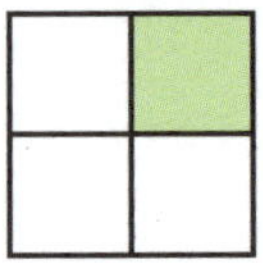 .... b)  ....

   2 marks

2. Complete the equivalent fractions for the fraction shaded in the shape.

   ☐/4   ☐/2

   2 marks

3. Complete the equivalent fractions for the fraction shaded in this shape:

   ☐/6   ☐/2

   2 marks

4. Tick the shapes that show the same fraction.

   1 mark

Challenge 2

1. Shade $\frac{1}{3}$ of this shape.

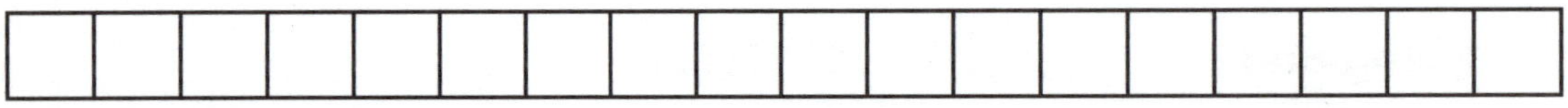

   1 mark

2. a) Shade $\frac{1}{4}$ of each shape.

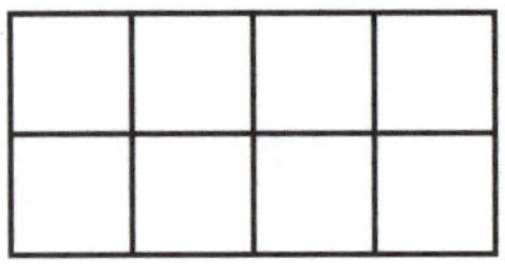

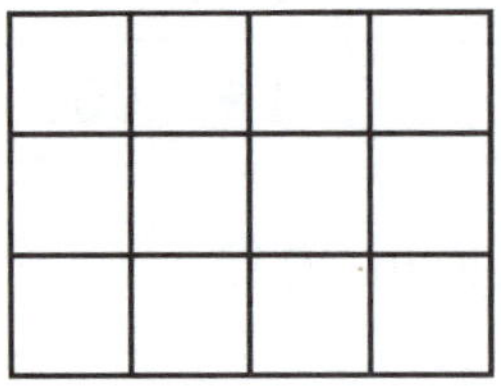

   2 marks

   b) Write two fractions that are equivalent to $\frac{1}{4}$

   .... and ....

   2 marks

3 This grid has 100 squares.

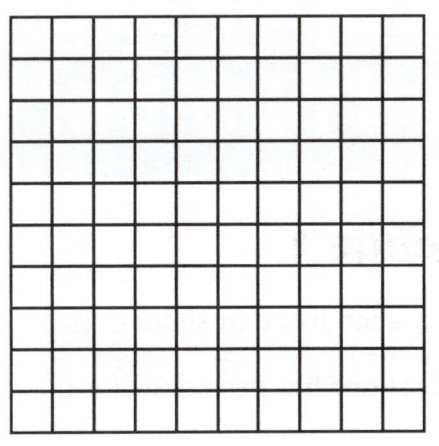

a) How many tenths are equivalent to 70 hundredths?

....

b) How many hundredths are equivalent to 2 tenths?

....

4 Circle the fractions that are equivalent to $\frac{1}{2}$

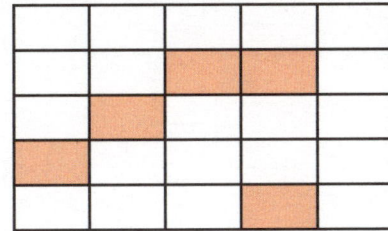

Challenge 3

1 What fraction of this shape is shaded?

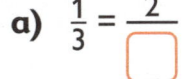 $\frac{1}{\Box}$

2 Complete these equivalent fractions.

a) $\frac{1}{3} = \frac{2}{\Box}$ b) $\frac{1}{2} = \frac{3}{\Box}$

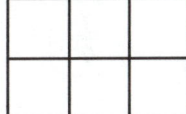

3 Shade $\frac{2}{5}$ of this shape.

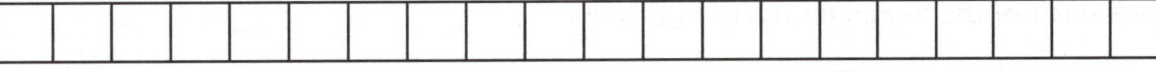

4 a) How many hundredths are equivalent to $\frac{1}{2}$? $\frac{\Box}{100}$

b) How many hundredths are equivalent to $\frac{1}{4}$? $\frac{\Box}{100}$

c) How many hundredths are equivalent to $\frac{3}{4}$? $\frac{\Box}{100}$

5 Complete these equivalent fractions.

a) $\frac{1}{6} = \frac{\Box}{12}$ b) $\frac{1}{4} = \frac{\Box}{12}$ c) $\frac{1}{3} = \frac{\Box}{12}$

d) $\frac{1}{2} = \frac{\Box}{12}$ e) $\frac{2}{3} = \frac{\Box}{12}$ f) $\frac{3}{4} = \frac{\Box}{12}$

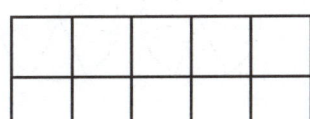

How am I doing?   Total marks: ☐ / 28

Fractions (including decimals)   37

Improper fractions and mixed numbers

Challenge 1

1 Write each fraction shaded as an improper fraction, and as a mixed number. The first one has been done for you.

		Improper fraction	Mixed number
a)	(2 full circles shaded in halves + 1 half shaded)	$\frac{5}{2}$	$2\frac{1}{2}$
b)	(1 circle shaded in quarters + 1 quarter shaded)	$\frac{\square}{\square}$	$\square\frac{\square}{\square}$
c)	(2 full circles in sixths + 4 sixths shaded)	$\frac{\square}{\square}$	$\square\frac{\square}{\square}$
d)	(bars shaded in fifths)	$\frac{\square}{\square}$	$\square\frac{\square}{\square}$

6 marks

2 a) Circle each of the improper fractions in this list.

$\frac{1}{2}$ $\frac{7}{4}$ $1\frac{3}{8}$ $\frac{7}{9}$ $2\frac{1}{5}$ $\frac{11}{6}$ $\frac{9}{5}$ $3\frac{1}{7}$

1 mark

b) Tick each of the mixed numbers in this list.

1 mark

Challenge 2

1 Circle each value that is greater than 1.

$\frac{1}{5}$ $\frac{7}{3}$ $1\frac{4}{5}$ $\frac{11}{9}$ $3\frac{1}{4}$ $\frac{5}{6}$ $\frac{12}{5}$ $\frac{11}{12}$

1 mark

2 a) Shade $\frac{11}{7}$

b) Write $\frac{11}{7}$ as a mixed number.

....

2 marks

3 a) Shade $\frac{27}{10}$

b) Write $\frac{27}{10}$ as a mixed number.

....

2 marks

38

4 Write each value shown on the number line as an improper fraction, and as a mixed number.

The first one has been done for you.

a)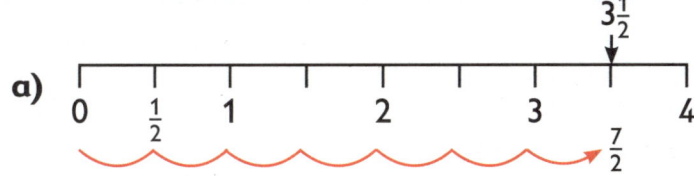

$\dfrac{7}{2}$

b)

c)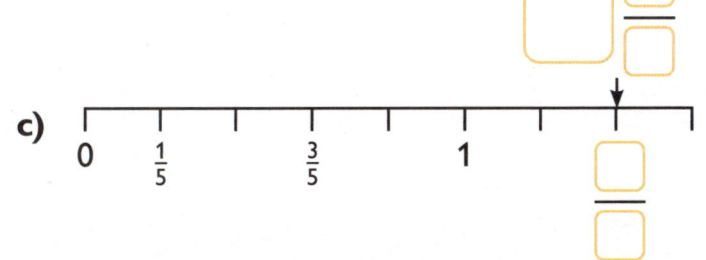

4 marks

Challenge 3

1 Write each fraction shaded as a mixed number with a unit fraction.

The first one has been done for you.

A unit fraction has 1 'on top'.

a) 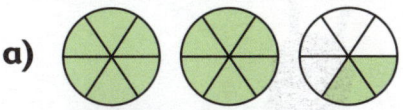 $1\dfrac{1}{3}$

b) 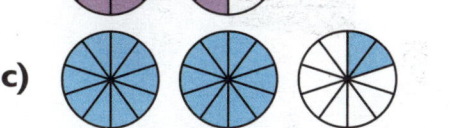 $\Box\dfrac{1}{\Box}$

c)  $\Box\dfrac{1}{\Box}$

2 marks

2 Draw lines to match each improper fraction to its equivalent mixed number.

$4\dfrac{3}{5}$ $8\dfrac{1}{10}$ $\dfrac{7}{3}$ $\dfrac{9}{2}$ $6\dfrac{4}{5}$ $\dfrac{11}{4}$ $\dfrac{29}{9}$

$\dfrac{34}{5}$ $2\dfrac{1}{3}$ $3\dfrac{2}{9}$ $\dfrac{81}{10}$ $\dfrac{23}{5}$ $4\dfrac{1}{2}$ $2\dfrac{3}{4}$

7 marks

How am I doing?   Total marks: ☐ /26

Fractions (including decimals) **39**

Comparing and ordering fractions

Challenge 1

1. Write these fractions in order, from smallest to largest.

   $\frac{1}{3}$ $\frac{1}{2}$ $\frac{1}{5}$ $\frac{1}{4}$ $\frac{1}{6}$ $\frac{1}{10}$

   smallest ☐ ☐ ☐ ☐ ☐ ☐ largest

   2 marks

2. Write < or > to make each statement correct.

   a) $\frac{3}{6}$ ☐ $\frac{5}{6}$ b) $\frac{8}{10}$ ☐ $\frac{9}{10}$

   c) $\frac{1}{5}$ ☐ $\frac{2}{5}$ d) $\frac{7}{8}$ ☐ $\frac{5}{8}$

   4 marks

Challenge 2

1. Write < or > to make each statement correct.

   a) 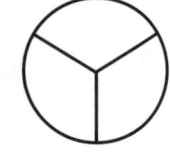 $\frac{5}{6}$ ☐ $\frac{2}{3}$

   b) 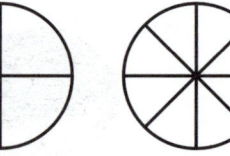 $\frac{3}{4}$ ☐ $\frac{5}{8}$

   c)  $\frac{7}{10}$ ☐ $\frac{3}{5}$

   3 marks

2. Write these fractions in order, starting with the smallest.

   $\frac{3}{10}$ $\frac{87}{100}$ $\frac{1}{10}$ $\frac{41}{100}$ $\frac{1}{100}$ $\frac{9}{10}$

   smallest ☐ ☐ ☐ ☐ ☐ ☐ largest

   2 marks

40

3. Write these fractions in order, starting with the largest.

$\frac{1}{4}$ $\frac{5}{8}$ $\frac{1}{2}$ $\frac{3}{4}$ $\frac{7}{8}$ $\frac{9}{16}$

largest ☐ ☐ ☐ ☐ ☐ ☐ smallest

2 marks

4. Circle the larger fraction in each pair.

a) $\frac{2}{5}$ $\frac{1}{4}$

b) $\frac{3}{5}$ $\frac{7}{8}$

c) $\frac{4}{6}$ $\frac{6}{8}$

d) $\frac{2}{5}$ $\frac{1}{3}$

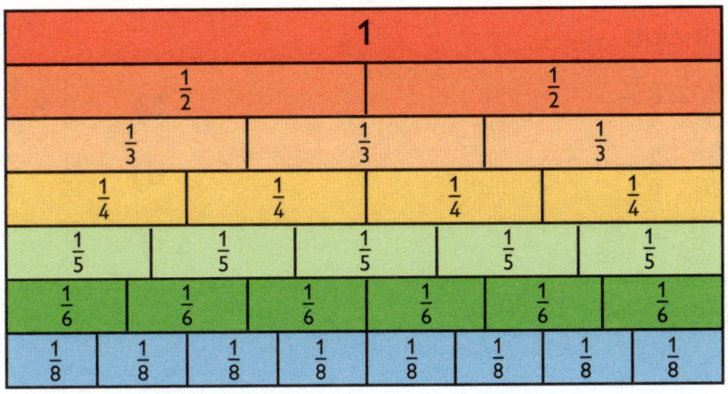

Use the fraction wall to help you.

4 marks

5. Write the missing numbers to make these statements true.

a) $\frac{\square}{3} > \frac{1}{2}$

b) $\frac{\square}{4} < \frac{7}{8}$

c) $\frac{3}{\square} < \frac{1}{2}$

d) $\frac{5}{\square} > \frac{3}{4}$

Use the fraction wall to help you.

4 marks

Challenge 3

1. Write these mixed numbers in order, starting with the smallest.

$2\frac{5}{6}$ $2\frac{2}{3}$ $3\frac{4}{5}$ $2\frac{3}{4}$ $3\frac{7}{10}$ $2\frac{5}{8}$

smallest ☐ ☐ ☐ ☐ ☐ ☐ largest

2 marks

2. Write these fractions and mixed numbers in order, starting with the smallest.

$3\frac{1}{3}$ $\frac{5}{3}$ $2\frac{1}{3}$ $\frac{9}{3}$ $\frac{2}{3}$ $2\frac{2}{3}$

smallest ☐ ☐ ☐ ☐ ☐ ☐ largest

2 marks

3. Lisa writes these fractions in order, starting with the smallest.

$\frac{1}{3}$ $\frac{3}{6}$ $\frac{11}{12}$ $\frac{5}{6}$ $\frac{8}{12}$ $\frac{1}{6}$

Which fraction is 4th in Lisa's list? ....

1 mark

4. Which of these fractions is closest to $\frac{1}{2}$?

$\frac{3}{8}$ $\frac{4}{6}$ $\frac{7}{12}$ $\frac{1}{3}$ $\frac{6}{10}$

....

1 mark

How am I doing?

Total marks: ☐ /27

Fractions (including decimals)   41

Adding and subtracting fractions

Challenge 1

1. Work out:
   a) $\frac{1}{4} + \frac{2}{4} =$ ....
   b) $\frac{2}{5} + \frac{1}{5} =$ ....
   c) $\frac{5}{8} - \frac{2}{8} =$ ....
   d) $\frac{13}{15} - \frac{9}{15} =$ ....
   e) $\frac{19}{100} + \frac{32}{100} =$ ....
   f) $\frac{11}{20} - \frac{4}{20} =$ ....

   6 marks

2. Work out:
   a) $1 - \frac{1}{4} =$ ....
   b) $1 - \frac{1}{5} =$ ....
   c) $1 - \frac{2}{7} =$ ....
   d) $1 - \frac{7}{10} =$ ....

   4 marks

3. Lucas eats $\frac{2}{3}$ of a pizza.

   What fraction of the pizza is left?

   ....

   1 mark

Challenge 2

1. Work out:
   a) $\frac{1}{4} + \frac{1}{8} =$ .... = ...
   b) $\frac{1}{5} + \frac{1}{10} =$ .... = ...
   c) $\frac{5}{8} - \frac{1}{4} =$ .... = ...
   d) $\frac{9}{10} - \frac{2}{5} =$ .... = ...
   e) $\frac{1}{2} + \frac{1}{8} =$ .... = ...
   f) $\frac{23}{100} - \frac{1}{10} =$ .... = ...

   6 marks

2. Write the answer to each calculation as an improper fraction.

   a) $\frac{1}{4} + \frac{7}{8} = \frac{\square}{8}$
   b) $\frac{4}{5} + \frac{3}{10} = \frac{\square}{10}$
   c) $\frac{9}{5} - \frac{1}{10} = \frac{\square}{10}$
   d) $\frac{7}{3} - \frac{5}{6} = \frac{\square}{6}$

   4 marks

3. Janan ate $\frac{1}{2}$ a melon.

   Ali ate $\frac{3}{8}$ of the same melon.

   What fraction of the melon was left? ....

   1 mark

4. Some children have these different containers filled with water.

$\frac{3}{10}$ litre $\qquad$ $\frac{4}{100}$ litres $\qquad$ $\frac{1}{5}$ litre

Do they have enough water in total to fill a 1 litre bottle? ....

1 mark

Challenge 3

1. Work out:

   a) $\frac{1}{4} + \frac{1}{2} - \frac{1}{8} =$ ....
   b) $\frac{5}{4} - \frac{1}{2} - \frac{1}{8} =$ ....
   c) $\frac{34}{100} + \frac{1}{5} - \frac{1}{10} =$ ....
   d) $\frac{1}{3} + \frac{1}{12} - \frac{1}{6} =$ ....

   4 marks

2. Write the answer to each calculation as a mixed number.

   a) $\frac{1}{2} + \frac{3}{4} =$ .... = ...
   b) $\frac{3}{5} + \frac{7}{10} =$ .... = ...
   c) $\frac{11}{4} - \frac{1}{2} =$ .... = ...
   d) $\frac{13}{6} - \frac{1}{3} =$ .... = ...

   4 marks

3. A jug contains $\frac{3}{4}$ of a litre of juice.

   Max pours $\frac{1}{8}$ of a litre into each of these glasses.

   What fraction of a litre of juice is left in the jug? ....

   1 mark

4. Circle two fractions in this list that add to $\frac{3}{4}$.

   $\frac{3}{6}$ $\frac{1}{3}$ $\frac{2}{5}$ $\frac{1}{4}$ $\frac{2}{9}$

   1 mark

5. Complete this table with the missing fractions.

Fraction	Fraction + $\frac{1}{2}$
$\frac{1}{8}$	
$\frac{5}{12}$	
	$\frac{13}{14}$
$\frac{7}{20}$	
	$\frac{9}{16}$

   5 marks

How am I doing?   Total marks: ____ / 38

Fractions (including decimals)

Multiplying fractions

Challenge 1

1. Work out:

   a) $3 \times \frac{1}{4} = $ ....

   b) $2 \times \frac{2}{5} = $ ....

   c) $5 \times \frac{1}{8} = $ ....

   d) $4 \times \frac{2}{9} = $ ....

   4 marks

2. Work out:

   a) $3 \times \frac{6}{100} = $ ....

   b) $9 \times \frac{7}{100} = $ ....

   c) $5 \times \frac{12}{100} = $ ....

   d) $6 \times \frac{11}{100} = $ ....

   4 marks

Challenge 2

1. Work out:

   a) $\frac{1}{4} \times 12$ ....

   b) $\frac{1}{5} \times 15 = $ ....

   c) $\frac{3}{4} \times 20 = $ ....

   d) $\frac{3}{8} \times 24 = $ ....

   4 marks

2. Complete these calculations.

   a) $2 \times 2\frac{1}{2} = $ ....   b) $3 \times 2\frac{1}{2} = $ ....

   c) $4 \times 2\frac{1}{2} = $ ....   d) $5 \times 2\frac{1}{2} = $ ....

   4 marks

3 Complete these calculations.

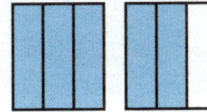

a) $2 \times 1\frac{2}{3} =$ ....

b) $3 \times 1\frac{2}{3} =$ ....

c) $4 \times 1\frac{2}{3} =$ ....

d) $5 \times 1\frac{2}{3} =$ ....

4 marks

Challenge 3

1 Work out:

a) $7 \times \frac{3}{1000} =$ ....

b) $12 \times \frac{9}{1000} =$ ....

c) $2 \times \frac{303}{1000} =$ ....

d) $3 \times \frac{111}{1000} =$ ....

4 marks

2 Write the answers as improper fractions and as mixed numbers.

The first one has been done for you.

a) $3 \times \frac{2}{5} = \frac{6}{5} = 1\frac{1}{5}$

b) $5 \times \frac{3}{8} =$ ....

c) $9 \times \frac{1}{4} =$ ....

d) $8 \times \frac{5}{7} =$ ....

e) $10 \times \frac{5}{8} =$ ....

f) $10 \times \frac{13}{100} =$ ....

g) $5 \times \frac{3}{10} =$ ....

h) $9 \times \frac{7}{5} =$ ....

7 marks

3 Write **<** or **>** to make each statement correct.

a) $3 \times \frac{1}{4}$ ☐ $\frac{5}{3} \times 2$

b) $6 \times \frac{5}{12}$ ☐ $\frac{7}{12} \times 5$

c) $6 \times \frac{7}{10}$ ☐ $\frac{1}{2} \times 8$

d) $7 \times \frac{3}{15}$ ☐ $\frac{5}{9} \times 4$

4 marks

4 I am thinking of a number.

$\frac{1}{4}$ of my number is 7.

What is $\frac{1}{2}$ of my number? ....

1 mark

5 I am thinking of a number.

$\frac{3}{4}$ of my number is 12.

What is $\frac{1}{2}$ of my number? ....

1 mark

How am I doing?

Total marks: ☐ / 37

Fraction and decimal equivalents

Challenge 1

1. Write the missing decimals on this number line.

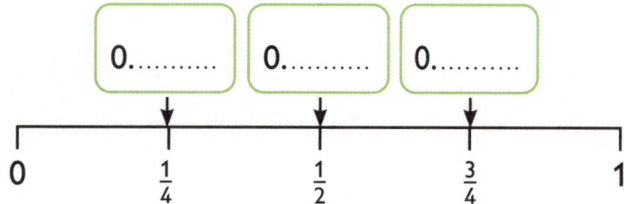

3 marks

2. Draw lines to match each fraction to its equivalent decimal.

   The first one has been done for you.

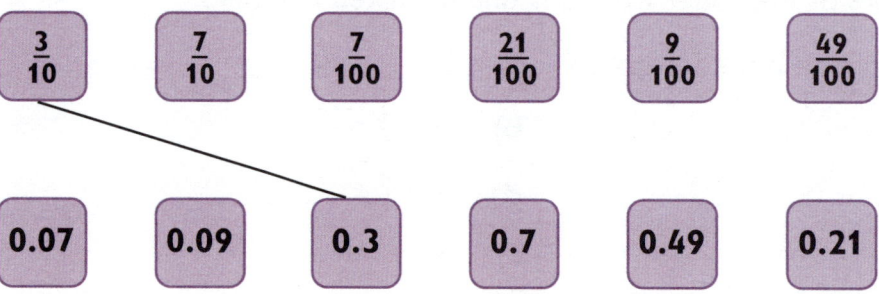

2 marks

Challenge 2

1. Complete the table.

   The first row has been done for you.

Words	Fraction	Decimal
1 hundredth	$\frac{1}{100}$	0.01
3 hundredths		
	$\frac{9}{10}$	
1 thousandth		
	$\frac{243}{1000}$	
13 hundredths		
		0.51
		0.129
7 thousandths		
		0.301

9 marks

46

2 Write in the missing numbers.

a) 0.1 = 0.10 = 0.100

$\frac{\square}{10} = \frac{10}{100} = \frac{\square}{1000}$

b) 0.3 = 0.30 = $\square$

$\frac{\square}{10} = \frac{30}{100} = \frac{300}{1000}$

c) 0.7 = $\square$ = 0.700

$\frac{\square}{10} = \frac{70}{100} = \frac{\square}{1000}$

d) 0.25 = 0.250

$\frac{\square}{100} = \frac{\square}{1000}$

e) $\square$ = 0.090

$\frac{9}{100} = \frac{\square}{1000}$

f) $\square$ = $\square$

$\frac{17}{100} = \frac{\square}{1000}$

3 Work out:

a) 2.3 × 10 = ...

b) 0.4 × 10 = ...

c) 1.6 × 100 = ...

d) 0.5 × 100 = ...

e) 9.2 × 1000 = ...

f) 6.81 × 1000 = ...

Challenge 3

1 Write < or > to make each statement correct.

a) 0.51 $\square$ $\frac{1}{2}$

b) 0.7 $\square$ $\frac{8}{10}$

c) 3.75 $\square$ $3\frac{1}{2}$

d) 0.3 $\square$ $\frac{15}{100}$

e) 0.84 $\square$ $\frac{8}{10}$

f) 0.059 $\square$ $\frac{6}{10}$

2 Work out:

a) 35 ÷ 10 = ...

b) 724 ÷ 10 = ...

c) 0.4 ÷ 10 = ...

d) 0.7 ÷ 100 = ...

e) 847 ÷ 100 = ...

f) 81 ÷ 1000 = ...

3 Write these decimals in order, starting with the smallest.

| 0.04 | 0.17 | 0.6 | 0.005 | 0.327 | 0.51 |

smallest ☐ ☐ ☐ ☐ ☐ ☐ largest

Rounding decimals

Challenge 1

1) Write each length to the nearest centimetre.

a)

.... cm

b)

.... cm

c)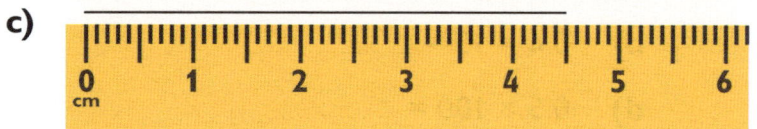

.... cm

3 marks

2) Round each decimal to the nearest whole number.

a) 4.6 ....
b) 6.2 ....

c) 12.9 ....
d) 8.5 ....

e) 23.4 ....
f) 99.8 ....

g) 992.5 ....
h) 999.7 ....

8 marks

Challenge 2

1) Round each price to the nearest pound.

a)
£1.85

£...............

b)
£1.55

£...............

c)
£7.50

£...............

d)
£2.20

£...............

e)
£1.15

£...............

f)
£4.79

£...............

6 marks

48

2 Use your rounded prices from question 1 to work out an estimate for the total cost of all the items.

£.................. *1 mark*

3 Round each decimal to the nearest whole number.

a) 7.18 .... b) 26.85 ....

c) 102.93 .... d) 5220.49 ....

e) 39 490.64 .... f) 932 555.55 ....

6 marks

4 Round each decimal to the nearest tenth.

a) 16.83 .... b) 29.48 ....

c) 73.56 .... d) 283.54 ....

e) 1304.62 .... f) 2047.75 ....

6 marks

Challenge 3

1 Mel rounds all these numbers to 1 decimal place.

9.61   9.58   9.55   9.63   9.65   9.59

Which number **does not** round to 9.6? ....

1 mark

2 Work out each calculation. Round each answer to 1 decimal place.

The first one has been started for you.

a) 6.25 + 5.34 = 11.59   rounded to 1 decimal place ....

b) 15.31 + 8.42 = ...   rounded to 1 decimal place ....

c) 24.86 − 5.14 = ...   rounded to 1 decimal place ....

d) 75.03 − 10.25 = ...   rounded to 1 decimal place ....

e) 120.46 × 2 = ...   rounded to 1 decimal place ....

f) 525 ÷ 100 ....   rounded to 1 decimal place ....

6 marks

3 A builder has a piece of wood 3 metres long.

He cuts the piece of wood into 8 equal pieces.

How long is each piece?

Give your answer to the nearest centimetre.

.... cm

1 mark

How am I doing?   Total marks: ☐ / 38

Fractions (including decimals)   **49**

Fractions, decimals and percentages

Challenge 1

1. Here is a 100 square.

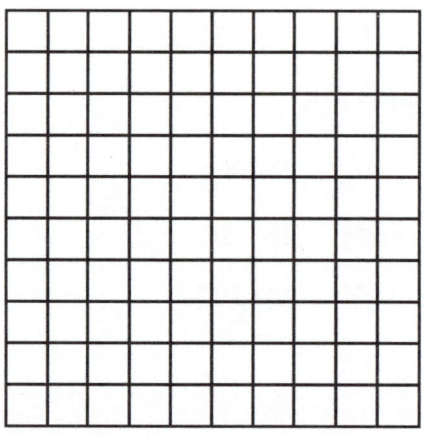

   a) Colour 10% of the 100 square yellow.

   b) Colour 25% of the 100 square green.

   c) Colour 1% of the 100 square blue.

   3 marks

2. Draw lines to match each percentage to its equivalent fraction.

   | 33% | 6% | 90% | 76% | 9% |

   | $\frac{90}{100}$ | $\frac{9}{100}$ | $\frac{33}{100}$ | $\frac{76}{100}$ | $\frac{6}{100}$ |

   2 marks

Challenge 2

1. Draw lines to match each percentage to its equivalent decimal.

   | 54% | 10% | 45% | 5% | 1% | 50% |

   | 0.5 | 0.45 | 0.01 | 0.54 | 0.1 | 0.05 |

   2 marks

50

2 Write the percentage shaded in each diagram.

a) ....% b) ....%

c) ....% d) ....%

e) ....% f) ....%

6 marks

Challenge 3

1 Circle the larger amount in each pair.

a) $\frac{1}{2}$ or 60%   b) $\frac{1}{4}$ or 20%

c) $\frac{9}{10}$ or 0.99   d) $\frac{1}{100}$ or 10%

e) 0.2 or 40%   f) $\frac{3}{4}$ or 70%

6 marks

2 Write these amounts in order, starting with the smallest.

30% $\frac{11}{25}$ 0.4 $\frac{1}{4}$ 42%

smallest ☐ ☐ ☐ ☐ ☐ largest

2 marks

3 Work out:

a) 50% of £20

£....................

b) 25% of 36 cm

....................cm

c) 75% of 28 grams

.... grams

d) 10% of £30

£....................

4 marks

How am I doing?   Total marks: ☐ /25

Fractions (including decimals)   **51**

Fraction, decimal and percentage problems

Challenge 1

1 Ethan has 60% of the money he needs for a new bike.

What percentage of the money does he still need?

.... 1 mark

2 Maria has 36 marbles.

Jacob has half as many marbles as Maria.

How many marbles do they have in total?

.... 1 mark

3 Circle two numbers which add to make 0.15

 0.1    0.5    0.7    0.08    0.05

1 mark

Challenge 2

1 One chair is 0.4 metres wide.

12 of these chairs are put side by side in a row.

How long is the row of chairs?

0.4m

.... metres   1 mark

2 In these addition pyramids, add two numbers to get the number in the space above.

Complete the pyramids.

a)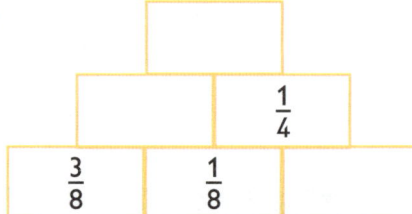

b) Top: $1\frac{2}{6}$, right: $\frac{5}{6}$, bottom-left: $\frac{1}{6}$

6 marks

52

3. Complete these number calculations.

 a) 84.6 ▢ = 0.846

 b) 17.85 ▢ = 178.5

4. Tina is making pizzas for a party.

 There will be 12 people at the party.

 Tina thinks each person will eat $\frac{3}{4}$ of a pizza.

 How many pizzas does Tina need to make for her party?

Challenge 3

1. Here are four numbers.

 Write each of these numbers once in this calculation to make it correct.

 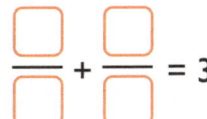 = 3

2. a) Round 346.57 to the nearest ten.

 b) Round 346.57 to the nearest tenth.

3. There are 60 people on a bus.

 $\frac{3}{4}$ of the people are adults.

 The rest are children.

 40% of the children are wearing glasses.

 How many children are wearing glasses?

How am I doing?   Total marks: ▢ /17

Fractions (including decimals)   53

Progress test 2

1. Work out:

    9347 − 468 = ...   **1 mark**

2. Complete the equivalent fractions for the fraction shaded in this shape.

    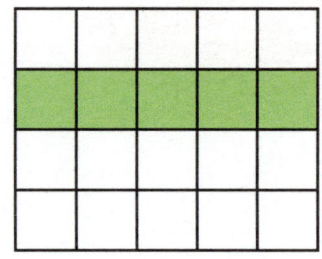

    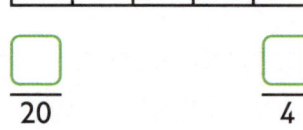

    2 marks

3. a) Write all the factors of 12.

    ....   **1 mark**

    b) Write the first four multiples of 12.

    ....   **1 mark**

4. This thermometer shows a temperature of 3°C.

    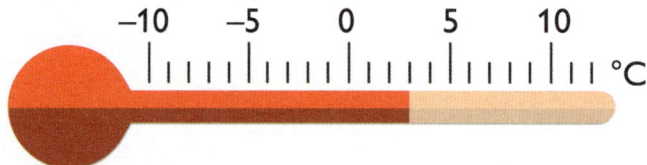

    The temperature falls by 7 degrees.

    What is the new temperature? ....°C   **1 mark**

5. Work out:

    $7 \times \frac{9}{100}$ = ...   **1 mark**

6. Layla spends 35% of her birthday money on books.

    What percentage of her birthday money does she have left?

    ....%   **1 mark**

7. Round 74 857:

   a) to the nearest ten. ....

   b) to the nearest hundred. ....

   2 marks

8. Work out:

   $\frac{5}{12} + \frac{6}{12} =$ ....

   1 mark

9. Write these temperatures in order, starting with the lowest.

   −9°C   23°C   8°C   −5°C   13°C   −27°C

   lowest [ ][ ][ ][ ][ ][ ] highest

   2 marks

10. Ivy eats $\frac{1}{5}$ of a cake.

    What fraction of the cake is left? ....

    1 mark

11. Write all the prime numbers less than 12.

    ....

    2 marks

12. Work out:

    a) 1.7 × 10 = ...   b) 0.3 × 1000 = ...

    2 marks

13. a) Shade $\frac{13}{5}$

    b) Write $\frac{13}{5}$ as a mixed number. ....

    2 marks

14. Round each decimal to the nearest whole number.

    a) 3.49 ....   b) 15.5 ....

    2 marks

15. What is the value of 3 in the number 534 879?

    ....

    1 mark

16. Work out:

    a) $\frac{4}{5} + \frac{1}{10} =$ ....   b) $\frac{7}{8} - \frac{1}{4} =$ ....

    2 marks

17. Shade $\frac{1}{3}$ of this shape.

    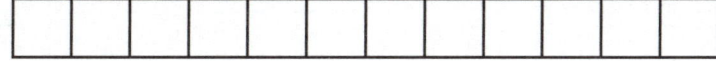

    1 mark

Progress test 2   55

18. Draw lines to match each percentage to its equivalent decimal.

| 35% | 10% | 4% | 1% | 40% |

| 0.4 | 0.01 | 0.35 | 0.1 | 0.04 |

2 marks

19. Write 1.5 as a mixed number. ....

1 mark

20. a) How many tenths are equivalent to 30 hundredths?

....

b) How many hundredths are equivalent to 6 tenths?

....

2 marks

21. Write the year MCMXCVII in numbers.

....

1 mark

22. Round each decimal to the nearest tenth.

a) 9.47 .... **b)** 12.72 ....

2 marks

23. Work out:

a) 7^2 = ...

b) 10^2 = ...

c) 2^3 = ...

3 marks

24. Write these fractions in order, starting with the smallest.

| $\frac{1}{2}$ | $\frac{7}{12}$ | $\frac{3}{8}$ | $\frac{3}{4}$ | $\frac{11}{12}$ |

smallest ⬜⬜⬜⬜⬜ largest

2 marks

25. Work out:

1428 × 24 =

....

1 mark

26. Write each fraction as a decimal.

a) $\frac{1}{4}$ = ... **b)** $\frac{1}{2}$ = ... **c)** $\frac{3}{4}$ = ...

3 marks

27. Work out:

a) $\frac{2}{5}$ × 15 = ...

b) $\frac{7}{8}$ × 32 = ...

2 marks

28. Five friends go on a boat trip.

The total cost is £344.

Work out how much each person pays.

Give your answer to the nearest pound.

£...................

29. Write each decimal as a fraction.

a) 0.53 = ...   b) 0.07 = ...   c) 0.829 = ...

30. Work out:

a) 83 ÷ 10 = ...   b) 1335 ÷ 100 = ...

31. Work out:

a) 50% of 30 kg

..................kg

b) 25% of £44

£..................

32. Write $2\frac{5}{8}$ as an improper fraction.   ....

33. Work out:

a) $2 \times 1\frac{1}{5} =$ ....   b) $4 \times 2\frac{2}{3} =$ ....

34. A charity looks after 180 animals.

60% of the animals are cats.

The rest of the animals are dogs.

a) How many dogs are there?

....

b) $\frac{1}{9}$ of the cats are black.

How many black cats are there?

....

35. Work out:

457 126 + 947 + 53 040 = ...

36. Here are some terms in a sequence.

47 225   47 885   48 545   ....

To get the next term you add the same number each time.

What is the first term greater than 50 000 in this sequence?   ....

How am I doing?   Total marks: .... / 60

Comparing measures

Challenge 1

1. Write these units in order of size, starting with the smallest.

   millimetre   metre   centimetre   kilometre

   smallest [___ | ___ | ___ | ___] largest

   2 marks

2. Complete these conversions:

   a) 1 m = ... cm   b) 1 cm = ... mm

   2 marks

3. Complete these conversions:

   a) 1 km = ... m   b) 1 kg = ... g

   c) 1 litre = ... ml

   3 marks

4. Write these measurements in centimetres.

   a) 4 m = ... cm   b) 6.5 m = ... cm

   c) 12 m = ... cm   d) 500 m = ... cm

   4 marks

Challenge 2

1. Write these measurements in metres.

   a) 500 cm = ... m   b) 350 cm = ... m

   c) 2000 cm = ... m   d) 45 cm = ... m

   4 marks

2. Convert these measurements into the units given.

   a) 2 litres = ... ml   b) 3.1 m = ... cm

   c) 5 kg = ... g   d) 3.2 litres = ... ml

   e) 24 km = ... m   f) 1.45 kg = ... g

   6 marks

3. Convert these measurements into the units given.

   a) 7500 ml = ... litres   b) 800 m = ... km

c) 500 g = ... kg d) 600 ml = ... litres

e) 1500 m = ... km f) 3250 g = ... kg

4 Approximately how much does a mug of tea hold?

Tick (✓) the correct answer.

300 litres ☐   3 ml ☐   300 ml ☐   3 litres ☐

5 Circle the heaviest sack of potatoes.

 900 kg    990 000 g    909 kg    9.9 kg

Challenge 3

1 Convert these measurements into the units given.

a) 15 ml = ... litres b) 35 cm = ... m

c) 25 g = ... kg d) 5 ml = ... litres

e) 1 m = ... mm f) 40 g = ... kg

2 Write < or > to make each statement correct.

a) 394 ml ☐ 0.4 litres   b) 6.3 km ☐ 630 m

c) 192 cm ☐ 1090 mm   d) 808 g ☐ 0.8 kg

e) 20 956 ml ☐ 209 litres   f) 1050 mm ☐ 10.5 m

3 Write these weights in order, starting with the smallest.

2.4 kg   20 g   0.2 kg   0.024 kg   400 g

smallest ☐ ☐ ☐ ☐ ☐ largest

4 A jug holds 1.75 litres of water.

a) How many 200 ml glasses can you fill from the jug of water? .... glasses

b) How much water is left over? .... ml

Perimeter

Challenge 1

1. Here is a rectangle on a 1 cm squared grid.

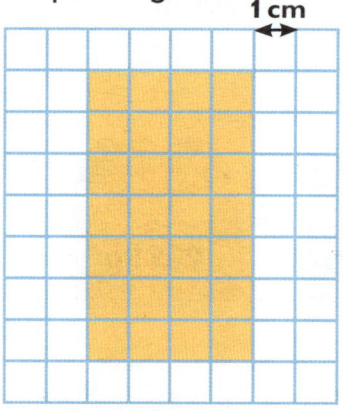

   What is the perimeter of this rectangle? .... cm

   1 mark

2. Work out the perimeter of this square.

   .... cm

   1 mark

3. Draw a rectangle with perimeter 18 cm on this 1 cm squared grid.

   1 mark

Challenge 2

1. Here is a shape on a 1 cm squared grid.

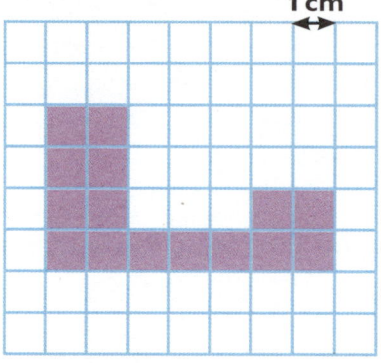

   What is the perimeter of this shape? .... cm

   1 mark

60

2. Work out the perimeter of this shape.

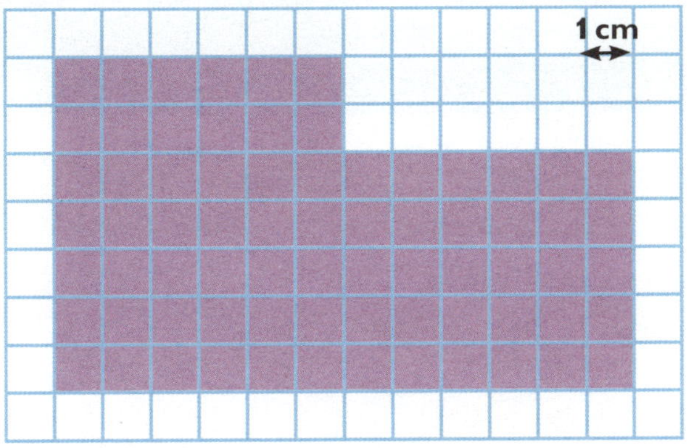

..................cm

1 mark

3. Calculate the perimeter of this square.

3.2 cm

Give your answer in millimetres. ....mm

1 mark

Challenge 3

1. Thea has made this T shape.

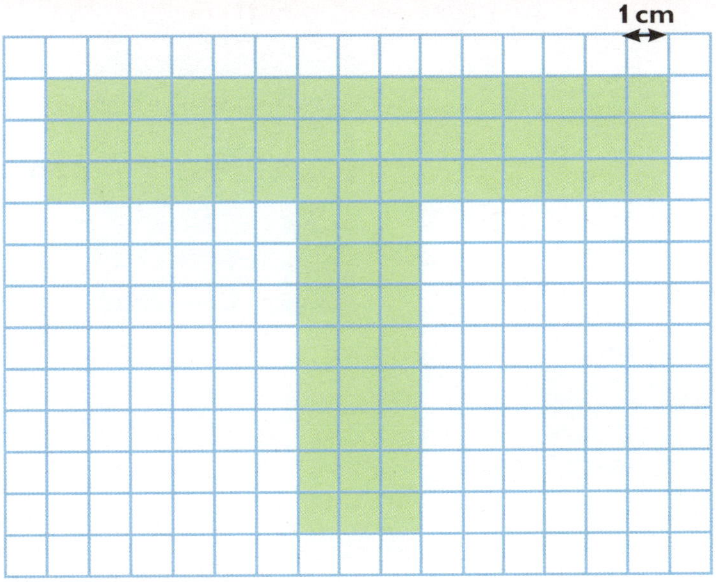

   She wants to put LED lights all around the perimeter of the T shape.

   LED lights come in 10 cm strips.

   How many strips of LED lights does Thea need?

   .... strips

1 mark

2. The perimeter of this rectangle is 7.4 metres.

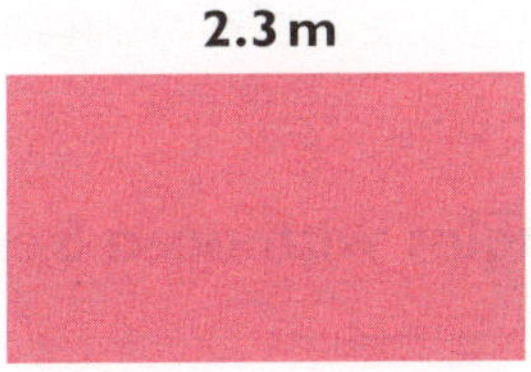

   2.3 m

   What is the width of this rectangle? ....m

1 mark

How am I doing? Total marks: ☐ / 8

Measures 61

Area

Challenge 1

1. Here is a rectangle on a 1 cm squared grid.

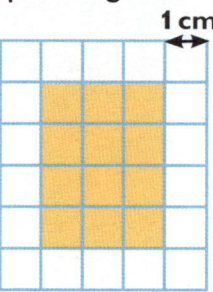

   What is the area of this rectangle? .... cm²

   1 mark

2. Calculate the area of each rectangle.

   a)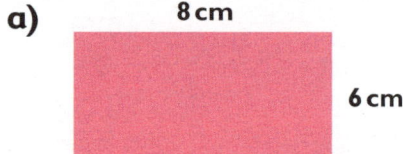

   ....

   b)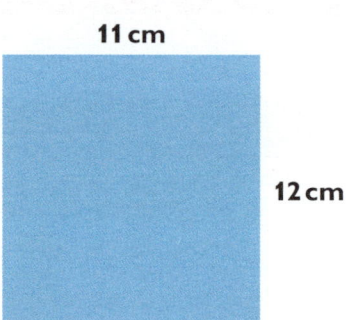

   ....

   c)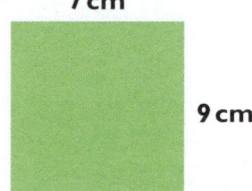

   ....

   3 marks

Challenge 2

1. Here is a 1 cm squared grid.

   On the grid, draw two different rectangles with area 8 cm².

   2 marks

62

② Convert the measurements of this rectangle to millimetres.

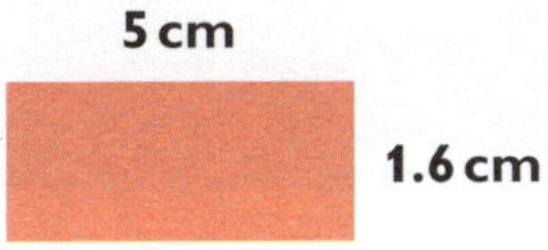

5 cm

1.6 cm

Work out the area of the rectangle in mm². .... 1 mark

③ $\frac{3}{4}$ of this rectangle is coloured blue.

36 cm² is coloured blue.

What is the area of the whole rectangle? .... 1 mark

Challenge 3

① The area of this square is 81 cm².

What is the perimeter of this square? .... 1 mark

② The school hall is a rectangle measuring 20 m by 35 m.

Max is painting the floor of the school hall.

The paint costs £15 per tin.

Each tin covers 25 square metres.

What is the total cost of the paint for the hall floor?

£.................... 3 marks

How am I doing? Total marks: ☐ /12

Measures

Time

Challenge 1

1 The time shown on this clock is in the afternoon.

Write the time shown:

a) as a pm time ....pm

b) using the 24-hour clock. ....

2 marks

2 The time shown on this clock is in the morning.

Write the time shown:

a) as an am time ....am

b) using the 24-hour clock. ....

2 marks

3 Draw the hands on this clock to show the time 00:09

1 mark

4 Luke makes sandwiches.

It takes him 3 minutes to make two sandwiches.

How many sandwiches can he make in 1½ hours?

....

1 mark

64

Challenge 2

1. Write < or > to make these time statements correct.

   a) 300 seconds ☐ 4½ minutes
   b) 450 minutes ☐ 7 hours
   c) 115 hours ☐ 5 days
   d) 2 days ☐ 2700 minutes
   e) 3 days ☐ 96 hours
   f) 2 weeks ☐ 340 hours

   6 marks

2. Four girls ran a 100 m race. The table shows their times.

Name	Time to run 100 m
Lisa	15.35 seconds
Flo	16.08 seconds
Sofia	17.51 seconds
Amy	15.2 seconds

   a) Who won the race? ....
   b) What is the difference between the fastest and slowest times? ....

   2 marks

Challenge 3

1. Lyn got on the train at 9.56 am.

   She got off the train at 11.13 am.

   How long was Lyn on the train? ....

   1 mark

2. Maggi started work at 9.45 am.

   She worked for 8 hours.

   After work, she walked 5 minutes to her mum's house and stayed there for 1½ hours.

   Then she walked 20 minutes to get home.

   What time did Maggi get home? ....

   1 mark

How am I doing?   Total marks: ☐ /16

Measures 65

Money

Challenge 1

1. Write these amounts of money in pounds.

   a) three pounds and twenty pence £..........................

   b) five pounds and four pence £..........................

   2 marks

2. One pencil costs 84p.

   How much do five of these pencils cost?
   Write your answer in pounds.

   £..........................

   1 mark

3. Round each amount to the nearest pound.

   a) £7.56 .... b) £3.40 ....

   2 marks

4. Maisie buys these clothes.

   Round each price to the nearest pound.

   a)  b)  c)

   £8.50   £6.20   £34.99

   £..............   £..............   £..............

   3 marks

5. Add your rounded prices from question 4 to work out an estimate for how much Maisie spends.

   £..........................

   1 mark

Challenge 2

1. A meal costs £74.
   Four people share the cost equally.
   How much does each person pay? £..........................

   1 mark

2. Work out:

   a) £8.83 × 100 = ... b) £8.83 × 1000 = ...

   c) £8830 ÷ 10 = ... d) £8830 ÷ 100 = ...

   4 marks

3. Seb makes 20 jars of jam.
   He spends £22.70 on fruit and sugar for the jam.
   He sells all the jars of jam for £2.40 each.

   How much money does he make? £..........................

   1 mark

4 Jackie earns £2400 each month.
She saves 10% of her earnings.

a) How much does she save each month?

£..........................

b) She spends $\frac{1}{3}$ of of her earnings on rent.

How much does she spend on rent?

£..........................

2 marks

Challenge 3

1 The table shows ticket prices for a water park.

Adult	£9.95	Over 65	£5.75
Child (aged 2–16)	£5	Under 2	£1.50
Family ticket (2 adults and up to 3 children)	£24		

a) Mr Patel is 68

His grandson is 12.

What is the total cost for their tickets for the water park?

£..........................

b) Mr and Mrs Smith have two children under 2.

Which is cheaper for them – a family ticket or two adult and two under 2 tickets?

....

c) What is the cheapest possible cost for 3 adults under 65 and 4 children aged between 10 and 14?

£..........................

3 marks

2 Carpet cost £16.50 per square metre.

How much do 30 square metres of this carpet cost?

£..........................

1 mark

3 5 kg of potatoes cost £2.75

How much do 3 kg of potatoes cost?

£..........................

1 mark

How am I doing?

Total marks: _____ /22

Measures 67

Volume and capacity

Challenge 1

1) The volume of this cube is 1 cm³.

Work out the volume of each of these shapes made from 1 cm³ cubes.

a)

.... cm³

b)

.... cm³

c)

.... cm³

d)

.... cm³

4 marks

Challenge 2

1) Estimate the volume of each cuboid.

a)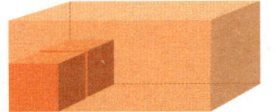

b)

.... cm³   .... cm³

2 marks

2) James pours water from the jug into the bucket.

It takes 9 jugs of water to fill the bucket.

Work out the capacity of the bucket, in litres.

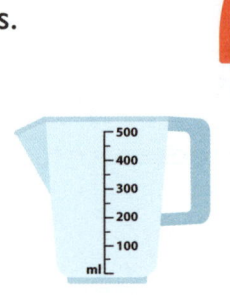 

.... litres

1 mark

68

3 Lois has a 1 litre carton of milk.

She pours out three 125 ml glasses of milk.

How much milk is left in the carton?

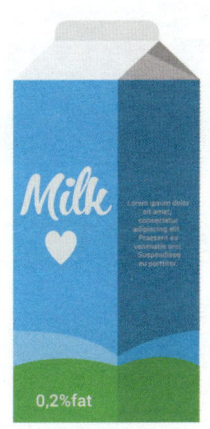

.... ml

1 mark

Challenge 3

1 a) Each side of this cube is 3 cm long.

How many 1 cm³ cubes does it take to make this cube?

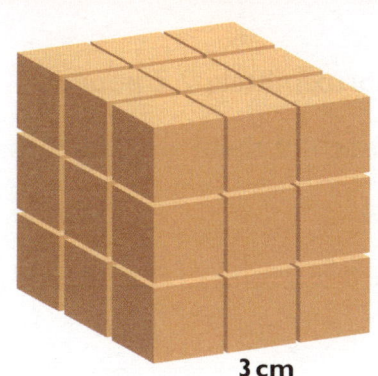

3 cm

....

b) Each side of this cube is 4 cm long.

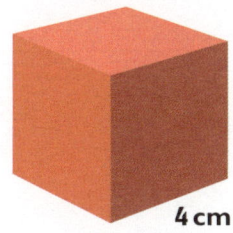

4 cm

How many 1 cm³ cubes does it take to make this cube? ....

2 marks

2 Shona uses this recipe to make a fruit drink.

Fruit drink

50 ml mango juice

200 ml apple juice

Shona wants to make 2 litres of fruit drink.

How much of each juice does she need?

Mango .... Apple ....

2 marks

How am I doing?   Total marks: ☐ /12

Measures 69

Metric and imperial units

Challenge 1

1 1 inch = 2.5 cm

Fill in the missing numbers on this double number line for inches and centimetres.

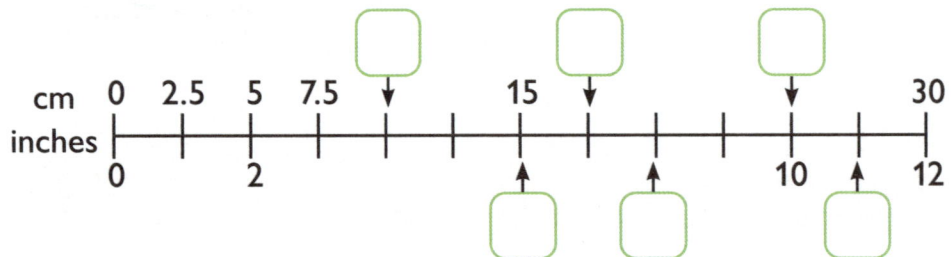

6 marks

2 1 kg is approximately 2.2 pounds.

Convert each of these weights into pounds.

a) 2 kg = ... pounds   b) 10 kg = ... pounds

c) 30 kg = ... pounds   d) 100 kg = ... pounds

4 marks

Challenge 2

1 There are 12 inches in 1 foot. 1 inch = 2.5 cm

Convert each of these lengths into centimetres.

a) 1 foot = ... cm   b) 5 feet = ... cm

c) $2\frac{1}{2}$ feet = ... cm   d) 60 feet = ... cm

4 marks

2 Write each measure under the correct heading.

inch   pint   centimetre   pound   gram   kilometre

litre   kilogram   foot   millilitre

Weight	Length	Volume or capacity

10 marks

70

3 1 pint is approximately 570 ml.

Convert each of these amounts into ml and litres.

a) 2 pints = ... ml = ... litres

b) 4 pints = ... ml = ... litres

c) 10 pints = ... ml = ... litres

6 marks

Challenge 3

1 There are 12 inches in 1 foot. 1 inch = 2.5 cm

Shanice is 5 feet 7 inches tall.
Milo is 163 cm tall.

a) Who is taller – Shanice or Milo?

....

b) How many cm taller?

....

2 marks

2 Write these units in order of size, starting with the smallest.

foot   inch   centimetre   metre

smallest [ ][ ][ ][ ] largest

2 marks

3 Write < or > to make each statement correct.

a) 1 kg ☐ 1 pound   b) 1 pint ☐ 1 litre

2 marks

4 1 gallon = 8 pints

1 pint = 570 ml

Convert 1 gallon to litres. ....

1 mark

5 1 litre = $1\frac{3}{4}$ pints

Write < or > to make each statement correct.

a) 3 litres ☐ 4 pints   b) 10 litres ☐ 18 pints

2 marks

How am I doing?   Total marks: ☐ /39

Measures 71

Scaling problems

Challenge 1

1. Bananas cost 30p each.

   How many bananas can you buy for £2? .... 1 mark

2. Here is a recipe for pasta sauce for 6 people.

   > 450 g tomatoes
   > 2 teaspoons tomato puree
   > 50 g onion
   > 1 tablespoon olive oil
   > 1 clove garlic

   a) Melissa makes pasta sauce for 12 people.

   How many grams of tomatoes does she need? ....

   b) Sandro makes pasta sauce for 30 people.

   How many grams of onion does he need? ....

   c) Linda makes pasta sauce for three people.

   How many teaspoons of tomato puree does she need? ....

   3 marks

Challenge 2

1. Daisy has a 1.5 kg block of cheese.

   She cuts the cheese into slices.

   Each slice weighs 175 g.

   She cuts as many 175 g slices as she can.

   How much cheese is left over?

   ....g   1 mark

2. A factory makes 24 pies every 5 minutes.

   How many pies does it make in 4 hours?

   ....   1 mark

3 The measuring jug contains the juice of three oranges.

How many oranges do you need to make 1 litre of juice? .... 1 mark

Challenge 3

1 Here are two cuboid shaped boxes.

Diagrams not drawn to scale.

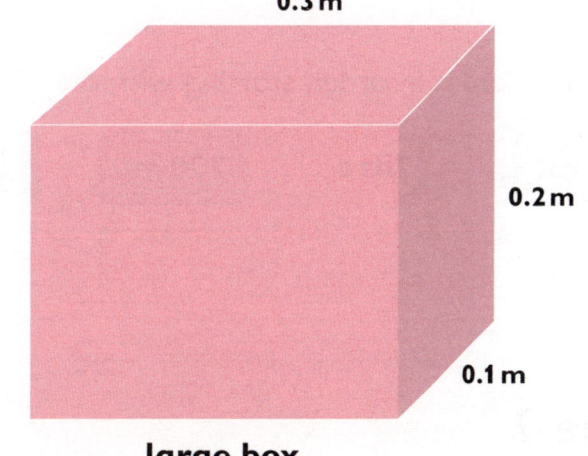

small box   large box

How many of the small boxes will fit into the large box?

.... 1 mark

2 A 25 g ball of wool costs £2.45

To knit a jumper you need 0.3 kg of wool.

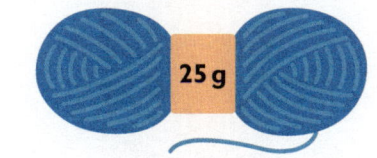

What is the total cost of the wool for this jumper?

.... 1 mark

3 A tap drips once every 5 seconds.

Each drip is 2 ml of water.

How many litres of water drip from the tap in 24 hours?

.... litres   1 mark

How am I doing?   Total marks: ☐ /10

Measures 73

Problem solving with measures

Challenge 1

1 Su has twenty 5p coins and thirty 10p coins.

How much money does Su have altogether?

.... 1 mark

2 Tyson is going to run a marathon, which is 26 miles.

9 people each sponsor him £3 for every mile he runs.

How much money will Tyson get when he completes the marathon?

.... 1 mark

3 Write these volumes in order, starting with the smallest.

800 ml $\frac{3}{4}$ litre   200 ml $\frac{1}{2}$ litre   60 ml

smallest [ ] [ ] [ ] [ ] [ ] largest

2 marks

Challenge 2

1 Milo builds a fence using these panels.

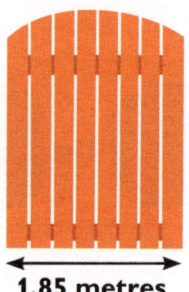
1.85 metres

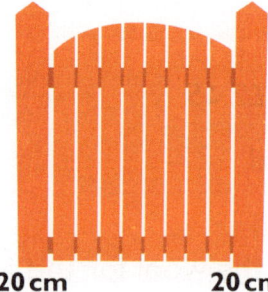
20 cm   20 cm

Each panel needs a post at each end.

Each post is 20 cm wide.

a) Milo makes a fence from eight panels.

How many posts does he use?

....

b) How long is Milo's fence, including the posts?

.... 2 marks

74

2 A puppy weighs half as much as its mother.
The puppy weighs 15 kg less than its father.
The puppy's father weighs 22 kg.

What is the weight of the puppy's mother?

.... 1 mark

3 1 kg = 2.2 pounds

Write these weights in order, starting with the smallest.

| 1 kilogram | 5 pounds | 4 kilograms | 1 pound |

smallest [ ] [ ] [ ] [ ] largest

2 marks

Challenge 3

1 Here is a plan of a playground.

The area of the playground is 192 m^2.

Mr Jones paints a white line all around the perimeter of the playground.

He can paint a line 8 m long with one tin of white paint.

Each tin of white paint costs £10.

How much does the paint for the whole perimeter cost?

.... 3 marks

2 Here is a rectangle.

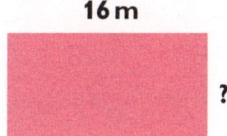

Four of these rectangles are used to make a frame.

a) What is the perimeter of the outside of the frame?

....

b) What is the shaded area inside the frame?

....

2 marks

How am I doing?   Total marks: [ ] / 14

Measures 75

Progress test 3

1. Here is a 100 square.

   10% of the 100 square is coloured blue.

   65% of the 100 square is coloured red.

   The rest of the 100 square is white.

   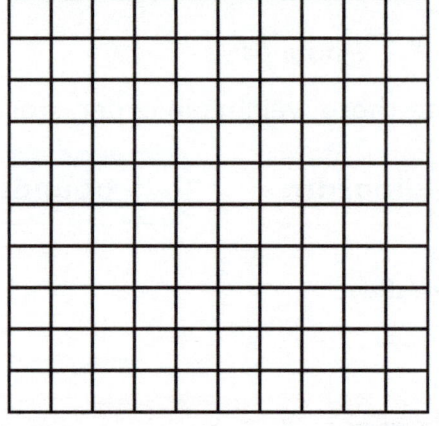

   What percentage of the 100 square is white? ....%

   1 mark

2. Work out:

   362 × 28 = ...

   1 mark

3. This clock shows a time in the evening.

   Write this time in 24-hour notation. ....

   1 mark

4. Write this year in numbers.

   MDXCIV ....

   1 mark

5. Write < or > in the box to make the statement correct.

   $\frac{5}{8}$ ☐ $\frac{3}{4}$

   1 mark

6. Write these measurements in grams.

   a) 4 kg = ... g

   b) 0.5 kg = ... g

   2 marks

7. Four cinema tickets cost £12.80

   How much is one ticket?

   .... 1 mark

8. Round 492.75 to:

   a) the nearest tenth. ....

   b) to the nearest ten. ....

   2 marks

9. Approximately how much does a teaspoon of sugar hold?

   Tick (✓) the correct answer.

   5 kg ☐   5 g ☐

   50 g ☐   0.5 kg ☐

   1 mark

10. Here is a diagram of a rectangular playground.

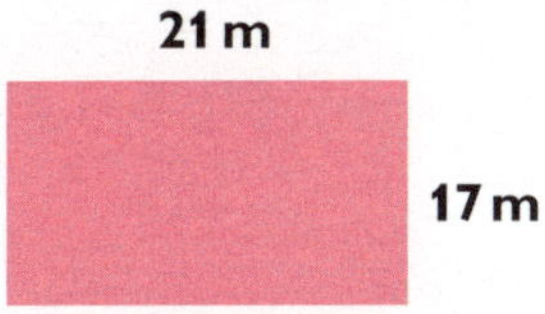

    21 m

    17 m

    a) Work out the area of the playground.

    .... m² 1 mark

    b) Work out the perimeter of the playground.

    .... m 1 mark

11. Write $\frac{29}{6}$ as a mixed number. .... 1 mark

12. Work out $\frac{4}{5}$ of 35 kg.

    .... kg 1 mark

13. The temperature starts at −3°C.

    It rises by 5 degrees and then falls 7 degrees.

    What is the final temperature?

    .... °C 1 mark

Progress test 3   77

14. Draw the hands on the clock to show the time 2 hours 20 minutes later than 16:52

1 mark

15. Convert these measurements into the units given.

   a) 5000 ml = ... litres   b) 430 cm = ... m

   c) 3 km = ... m   d) 520 mm = ... cm

4 marks

16. Six train tickets to London cost £102.

   How much do five train tickets to London cost?

   £.......................

1 mark

17. Work out:

   a) $5^2 + 12^2$ = ...   b) $9^2 - 2^3$ = ...

2 marks

18. Darius is painting a wall. The wall is a rectangle.

   The wall measures 9 m × 5 m.

   1 tin of paint covers 4 m²

   How many tins of paint does Darius need?

   ....

1 mark

19. Write < or > in the box to make the statement correct.

   15 weeks ▢ 108 days

1 mark

20. What are all the common factors of 36 and 30?

   ....

1 mark

21. Write the answer to each calculation as an improper fraction.

   a) $\frac{3}{4} + \frac{5}{8} = \frac{\square}{8}$ b) $\frac{6}{10} + \frac{3}{5} = \frac{\square}{10}$

2 marks

22. Circle all the cube numbers in this grid.

1	2	3	4	5	6	7	8	9	10
11	12	13	14	15	16	17	18	19	20

1 mark

23. Esme holds a cake sale for charity.

She sells small cakes for 50p each and large cakes for £2.50 each.

Esme sells 28 large cakes.

How many small cakes does she need to sell to make a total of £100?

....

1 mark

24. Work out:

a) $\frac{1}{2} + \frac{3}{4} - \frac{3}{8} =$ ....

b) $\frac{11}{12} - \frac{1}{2} - \frac{1}{6} =$ ....

2 marks

25. Dawn does 45 minutes of piano practice each day.

How many days does it take her to do 21 hours of practice in total?

.... days

1 mark

26. School starts at 08:40 and ends at 15:10

How long is the school day?   .... hours .... minutes

1 mark

27. Class 5 have 2 hours and 15 minutes of maths each week.

The school year is 43 weeks.

How many hours and minutes of maths do they have in a school year?

.... hours .... minutes

1 mark

28. Nish has two bags of 20p coins.

Bag A contains £5 worth of 20p coins and weighs 125 grams.

Bag B weighs 75 grams.

What is the total value of the coins in bag B?

....

1 mark

29. AA taxis charge £15 for a 4-mile journey.

BC taxis charge £24 for a 7-mile journey.

Which taxi firm charges the lowest amount per mile?

....

1 mark

How am I doing?   Total marks: [ ] /38

Progress test 3

Types of angle

Challenge 1

1 Draw lines to match each angle to its name.

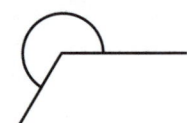   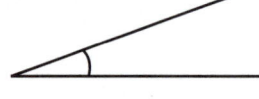   

acute   obtuse   reflex

3 marks

2 Measure the size of each angle.

a) 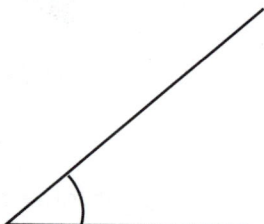   b)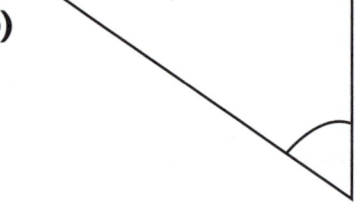

....

2 marks

3 Here is a trapezium.

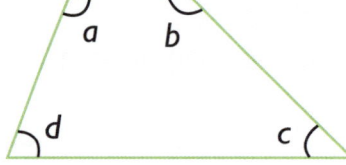

a) Write down the letter of the largest angle. ....

b) Write down the letter of the smallest angle. ....

2 marks

Challenge 2

1 What is the size of the shaded angle?

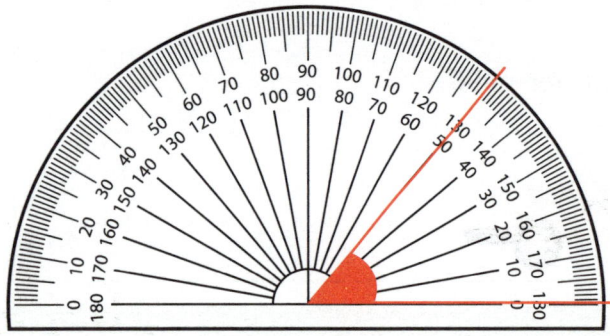

....

1 mark

80

2 Using the base line given, draw an angle of 70°

_____

1 mark

3 Using the base line given, draw an angle of 150°

_____

1 mark

Challenge 3

1 Measure the two acute angles in this triangle.

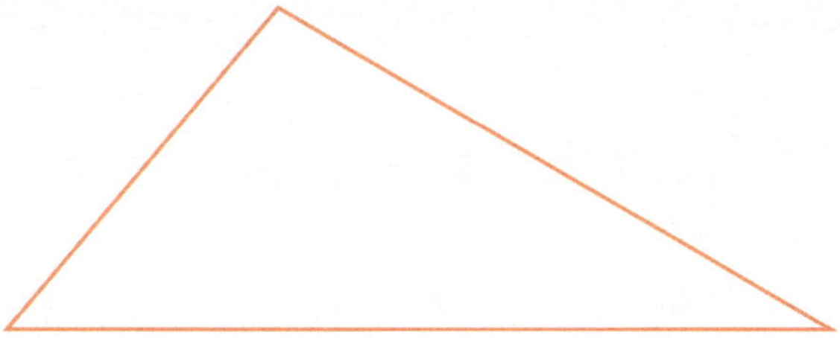

.... and ....

2 marks

2 Write these angles in the correct spaces in the table:

70°   200°   90°   140°

Acute	Obtuse	Reflex	Right angle

4 marks

3 Measure the largest angle in this hexagon.

....

1 mark

How am I doing?   Total marks: ☐ /17

Geometry – properties of shapes   81

Calculating angles

Challenge 1

1. Angle *a* and angle *b* make a straight line.

   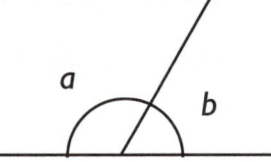

   What do two angles on a straight line add up to? ....° 1 mark

2. Work out the size of angle *d*.

   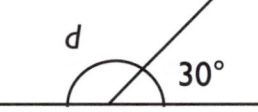

   ....° 1 mark

3. Work out the size of angle *g*.

   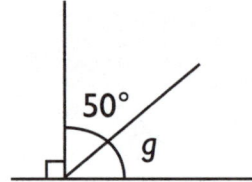

   ....° 1 mark

Challenge 2

1. Calculate the size of the acute angle in this diagram.

   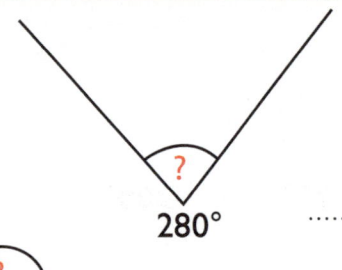

   ....° 1 mark

2. Calculate the size of the reflex angle in this diagram.

   ....° 1 mark

3. How many degrees does the minute hand of a clock turn through in 1 hour?

   ....° 1 mark

4. Three **equal** angles make a straight line.

   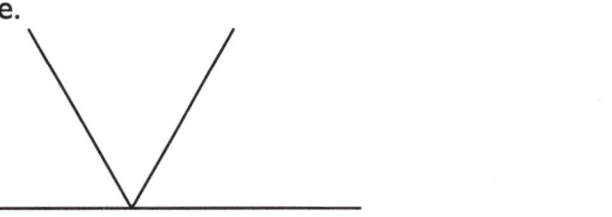

   What is the size of one of these angles? ....° 1 mark

82

5 Using the base line given, draw an angle of 330°

_____

1 mark

Challenge 3

1 This circle is divided into five equal parts.

Work out the size of angle n. ....°

1 mark

2 Work out the size of angle m.

55°   m

.................°

1 mark

3 How many degrees does the minute hand of a clock turn through from 8.20 am to 9.05 am?

.................°

1 mark

4 Here is a plan of a room.

window
sofa   table
door

a) Maisie stands facing the window.

How many degrees does she need to turn to face the door? ....°

b) Leroy stands facing the sofa.

How many degrees clockwise does he need to turn to face the door? ....°

c) Callie stands facing the table. She turns 90° anticlockwise.

What is she facing now? ....

3 marks

How am I doing?   😊   Total marks: ____ / 14

Geometry – properties of shapes   83

Polygons

Challenge 1

1) Draw all the lines of symmetry on these polygons.

3 marks

2) Here are some polygons.

    A   B   C   D   E

Write down the letters of:

a) the two pentagons. .... and ....

b) the two octagons. .... and ....

c) the hexagon. ....

d) the three regular polygons. .... and .... and ....

8 marks

Challenge 2

1) Draw a line from each shape to the correct word to show whether the polygon is regular or irregular.

regular   irregular

   B   C      

A   B   C   D   E   F

6 marks

2) Which type of triangle is a regular polygon?

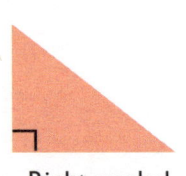      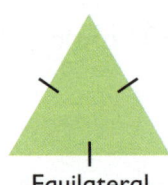 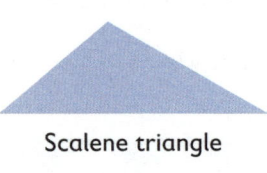

Right-angled triangle   Isosceles triangle   Equilateral triangle   Scalene triangle

....

1 mark

3 Complete the following sentences.

a) In a regular polygon, all angles are ....

b) In a regular polygon, all sides are .... length.

Challenge 3

1 Here is a rectangle.

Explain why this rectangle is **not** a regular polygon.

....

....

2 This polygon has 6 equal sides.

Explain why it is **not** a regular hexagon.

....

....

3 A regular polygon has 8 equal sides.

How many equal angles does the polygon have? ....

4 What fraction of this regular octagon is shaded?

....

Geometry – properties of shapes

2-D shapes

Challenge 1

1) Write ticks (✓) and crosses (✗) in this table to complete it correctly.

Two have been done for you.

Shape	It is a quadrilateral	It has some parallel sides
	✓	
		✗

8 marks

Challenge 2

1) Here are some shapes.

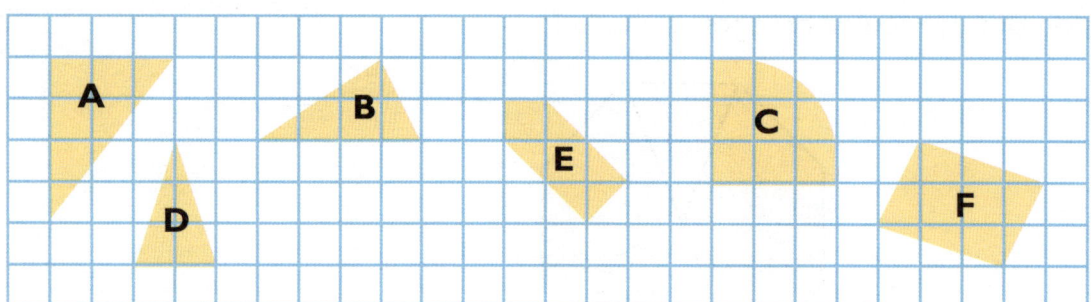

a) Which shapes have at least one right angle? ....

b) Which shapes have only acute angles? ....

c) Which shape has 2 parallel sides and 3 right angles? ....

3 marks

86

2 Here are some quadrilaterals.

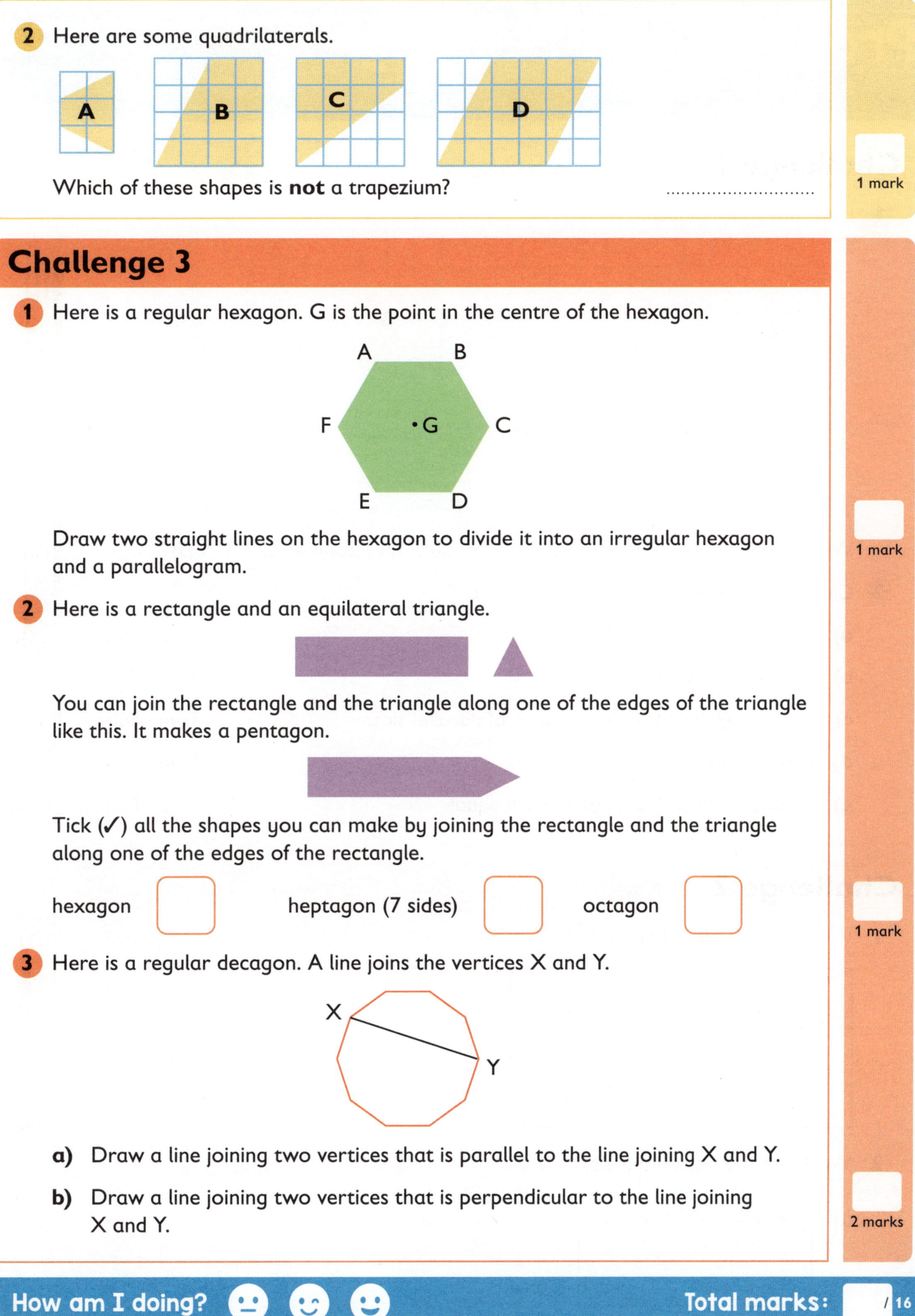

Which of these shapes is **not** a trapezium? .... 1 mark

Challenge 3

1 Here is a regular hexagon. G is the point in the centre of the hexagon.

Draw two straight lines on the hexagon to divide it into an irregular hexagon and a parallelogram.

1 mark

2 Here is a rectangle and an equilateral triangle.

You can join the rectangle and the triangle along one of the edges of the triangle like this. It makes a pentagon.

Tick (✓) all the shapes you can make by joining the rectangle and the triangle along one of the edges of the rectangle.

hexagon ☐   heptagon (7 sides) ☐   octagon ☐

1 mark

3 Here is a regular decagon. A line joins the vertices X and Y.

a) Draw a line joining two vertices that is parallel to the line joining X and Y.

b) Draw a line joining two vertices that is perpendicular to the line joining X and Y.

2 marks

How am I doing? 😐 😊 😃   Total marks: ☐ / 16

Geometry – properties of shapes   87

Properties of rectangles

Challenge 1

1. Here are some shapes.

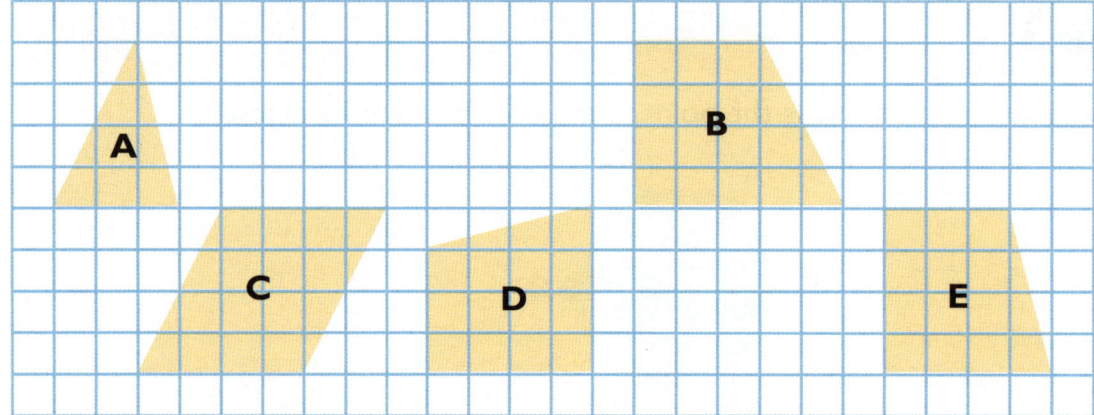

   Which two of these shapes fit together to make a rectangle? .... and ....

   1 mark

2. Circle **True** or **False** for each statement.

   a) A rectangle is a 3-D shape. — True / False

   b) A rectangle is a quadrilateral. — True / False

   c) A rectangle has exactly one pair of parallel sides. — True / False

   d) A rectangle has four right angles. — True / False

   e) Opposite sides of a rectangle are equal. — True / False

   5 marks

Challenge 2

1. Work out the size of angle *a*.

   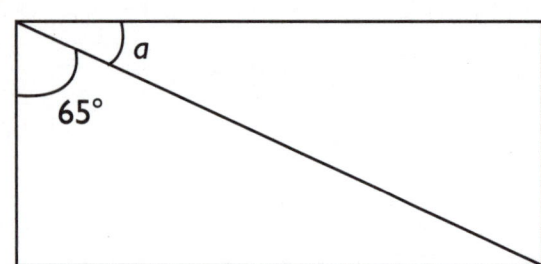

   ....° *1 mark*

2. Work out the size of angle *b*.

   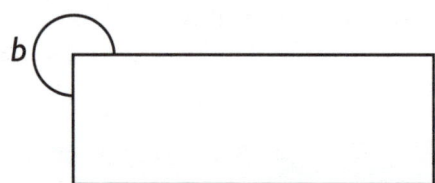

   ....° *1 mark*

3. Here is a square.

The line from A to C cuts the square exactly in half.

What is the size of angle *n*? ....°

1 mark

Challenge 3

1. Jacob has four of these rectangles.

   4 cm
   3 cm

   He joins the rectangles together to make this shape.

   a) What is the area of this shape? ....

   b) What is the perimeter of this shape? ....

   2 marks

2. This rectangle is cut along the diagonal line to make two identical triangles.

   25°

   a) The two triangles are joined to make this triangle.

   Work out the size of angle *m*. ....°

   b) The two triangles are joined to make this triangle.

   Work out the size of angle *y*. ....°

   2 marks

How am I doing?

Total marks: / 13

Geometry – properties of shapes   89

Properties of triangles

Challenge 1

1 a) Draw all the lines of symmetry on the triangles.

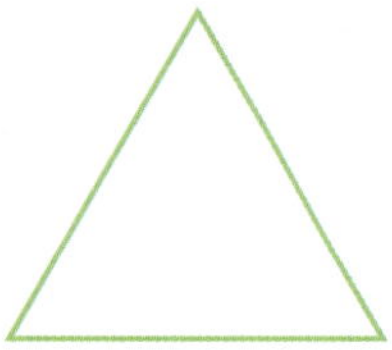

equilateral triangle   isosceles triangle

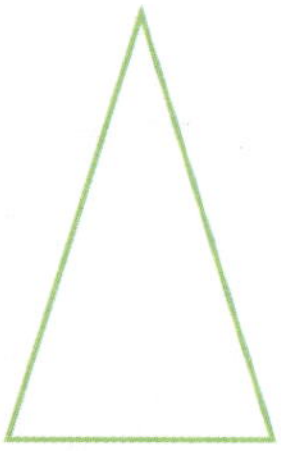

b) Tick (✓) the equal angles in the equilateral triangle.

c) Mark the equal angles in the isosceles triangle with a cross (✗).

4 marks

2 This equilateral triangle is cut in half to make two new triangles.

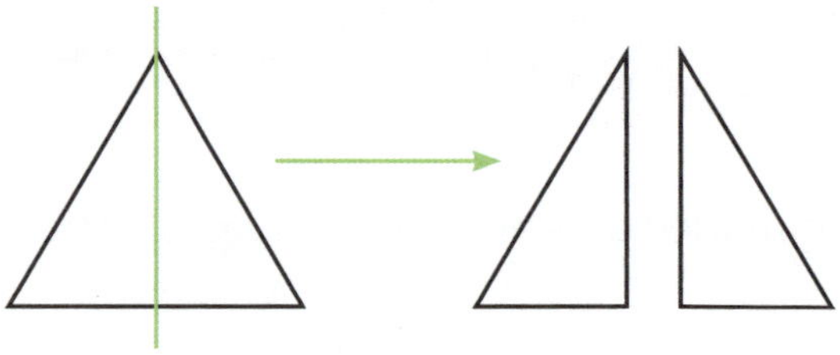

What type of triangle are the two new triangles? ....

1 mark

Challenge 2

1 Here is a triangle.

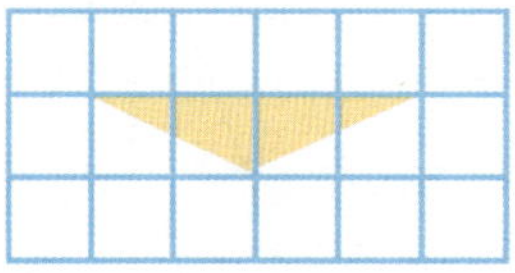

Tick (✓) all the statements that are true for this triangle.

two equal sides ☐   one right angle ☐

one obtuse angle ☐   two equal angles ☐

three equal angles ☐ isosceles ☐   equilateral ☐

2 marks

2 Here is a triangle.

Tick (✓) all the statements that are true for this triangle.

two acute angles ☐   one right angle ☐

one obtuse angle ☐   no equal sides ☐

three equal angles ☐   isosceles ☐   scalene ☐

2 marks

3 Here are some words used to describe triangles.

| acute | obtuse | right-angled | scalene | isosceles |

a) Use two of the words in the box to describe this triangle.

....

1 mark

b) Use two of the words in the box to describe this triangle.

....

1 mark

Challenge 3

1 Work out the size of angle *a*. Do not use a protractor.

.... °

1 mark

2 a) Draw a straight line on this kite to divide it into two scalene triangles.

b) Draw a straight line on this kite to divide it into two isosceles triangles.

2 marks

How am I doing?   Total marks: ☐ /14

Geometry – properties of shapes   91

3-D shapes

Challenge 1

1 Draw lines to match each of these 3-D shapes to its name.

a)  [cone shape] — triangular prism

b)  [cylinder shape] — cone

c)  [pyramid shape] — cylinder

d)  [triangular prism shape] — square-based pyramid

4 marks

Challenge 2

1 a) What is the name of this 3-D shape?

....

b) What shape are the faces of this 3-D shape? ....

2 marks

2 Liam has three identical bricks like this:

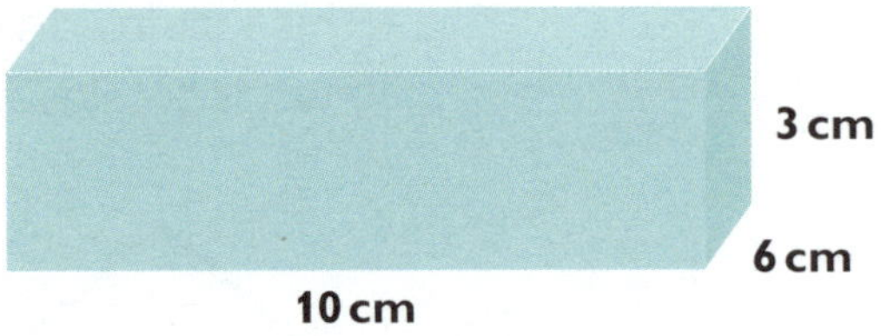

3 cm
6 cm
10 cm

He puts all three bricks one on top of the other to make a tower.

a) What is the height of the tallest tower he can make? .... cm

b) What is the height of the shortest tower he can make? .... cm

2 marks

3 What is the mathematical name for the shape of a ball? ....

1 mark

92

Challenge 3

1 Jodie makes this solid shape from 1 cm cubes.

How many more 1 cm cubes does Jodie need to make a cube with sides 3 cm long?

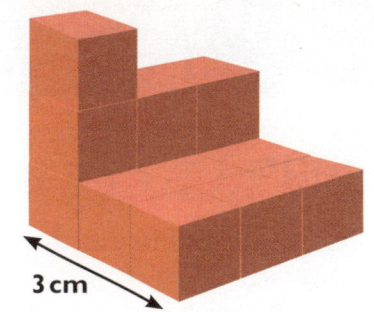

....

1 mark

2 A bird flies over some 3-D shapes.

The bird sees a shape that looks like this, from above.

Write the names of two 3-D shapes this could be.

.... and ....

2 marks

3 Here is a cuboid.

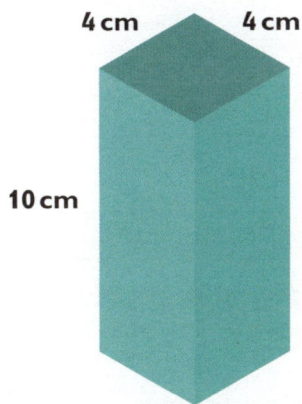

A cube with sides 4 cm is cut off the top of this cuboid.

a) Write the name of the 3-D shape that is left. ....

b) What is the length of the longest edge of this 3-D shape? ....

2 marks

4 Write the name of:

a) a 3-D shape with 4 triangular faces and one square face.

....

b) a 3-D shape with 4 triangular faces.

....

c) a 3-D shape with 2 triangular faces and 3 rectangular faces.

....

3 marks

How am I doing?   Total marks: / 17

Geometry – properties of shapes   93

Coordinates

Challenge 1

1. a) Plot these points on the grid.   (3, 5)   (4, 9)   (6, 9)   (5, 5)

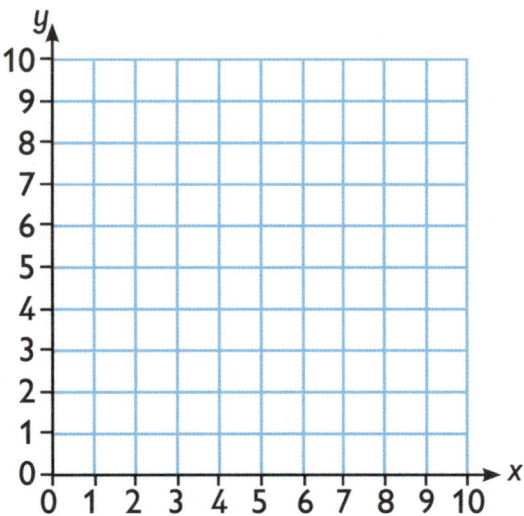

   b) Join the points in order with straight lines.

   What shape have you drawn? ....

   3 marks

Challenge 2

1. These coordinates are three vertices of a rectangle.

   A vertex is a corner. A rectangle has 4 vertices.

   (2, 2)   (7, 4)   (7, 2)

   a) Plot the points on the grid.

   b) What are the coordinates of the fourth vertex?

   (.................., ...)

   2 marks

94

2 These coordinates are three vertices of a rectangle.

(6, 5)   (6, 1)   (4, 1)

What are coordinates of the fourth vertex?   (............, ...)

2 marks

3 a) Line A is a straight line joining (2, 1) to (2, 7).

What are the coordinates of the midpoint of line A?   (............, ...)

b) Line B is a straight line joining (8, 3) to (3, 3).

What are the coordinates of the midpoint of line B?   (............, ...)

4 marks

Challenge 3

1 a) These coordinates are three vertices of a rhombus. (2, 3)   (3, 5)   (4, 4)

What are the coordinates of the fourth vertex?   (............, ...)

b) These coordinates are three vertices of a square. (4, 1)   (1, 4)   (4, 7)

What are the coordinates of the fourth vertex?   (............, ...)

4 marks

2 A rectangle is drawn on a 1 cm squared coordinate grid.

The vertices of the rectangle are at: (7, 6)   (3, 6)   (3, 8)   (7, 8)

Work out:

a) the perimeter of this rectangle.   ....

b) the area of this rectangle.   ....

2 marks

3 Line D is a straight line joining (1, 2) to (7, 8).

What are the coordinates of the midpoint of line D?   (............, ...)

2 marks

4 Jackie has plotted three vertices of a parallelogram.

Write down the coordinates of two different points that could be the fourth vertex of this parallelogram.

(............, ...)

or

(............, ...)

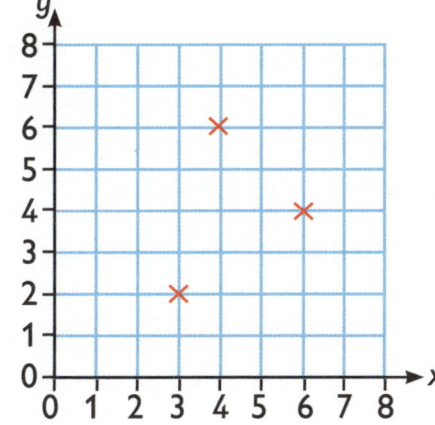

4 marks

How am I doing?   Total marks: .... / 23

Geometry – properties of shapes

Translations

Challenge 1

1 Triangle A is translated on to triangle B.

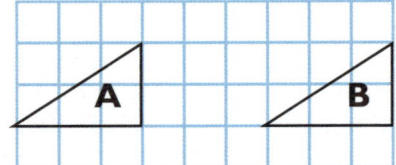

Complete the sentence.

Triangle B is translated .... squares right.

1 mark

2 Shape C is translated on to shape D.

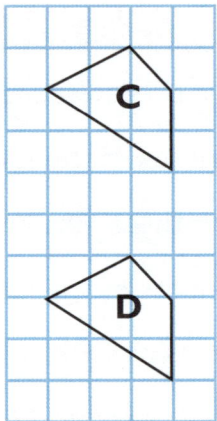

Describe the translation.

.... squares ....

2 marks

Challenge 2

1 Shape F is translated on to shape G.

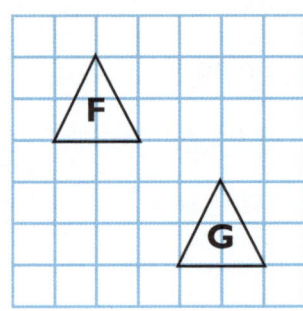

Describe the translation.

....

2 marks

2 Shape H is translated 3 squares up.

Draw shape H in its new position.

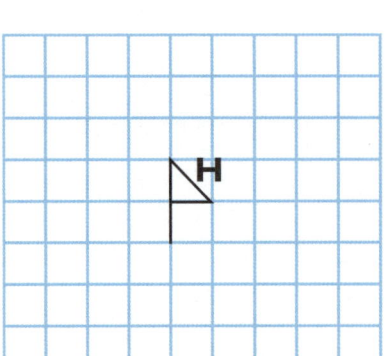

1 mark

96

3 a) Translate trapezium K
2 squares left
and
1 square down.

Label the translated shape J.

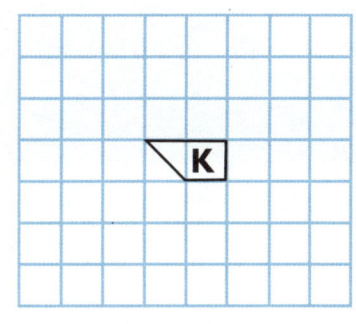

b) Describe the translation that takes shape J on to shape K.

....

2 marks

Challenge 3

1 This shape is translated so that point A moves to point B.

Draw the shape in its new position. Use a ruler.

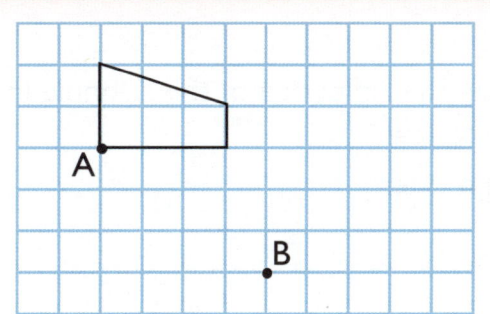

1 mark

2 Shape P is translated 5 squares right and 1 square up on to shape Q.

Shape Q is translated 1 square left and 4 squares down on to shape R.

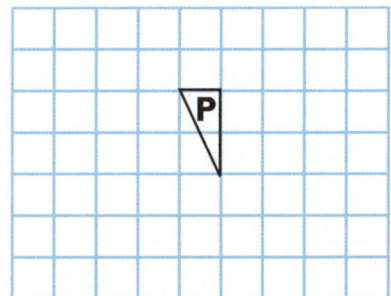

Describe the translation that takes shape R to shape P.

....

2 marks

3 Shape S is translated 2 squares right and 1 square up.

Draw the shape in its new position. Use a ruler.

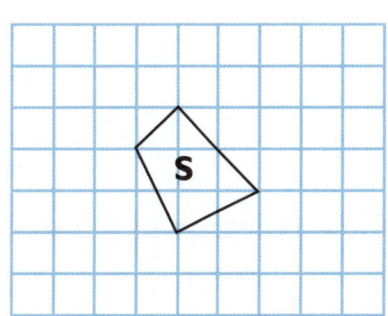

1 mark

How am I doing?   Total marks: ⬜ / 12

Geometry – properties of shapes   97

Reflections

Challenge 1

1. Tick (✓) the diagram that shows the correct reflection of the triangle in the mirror line.

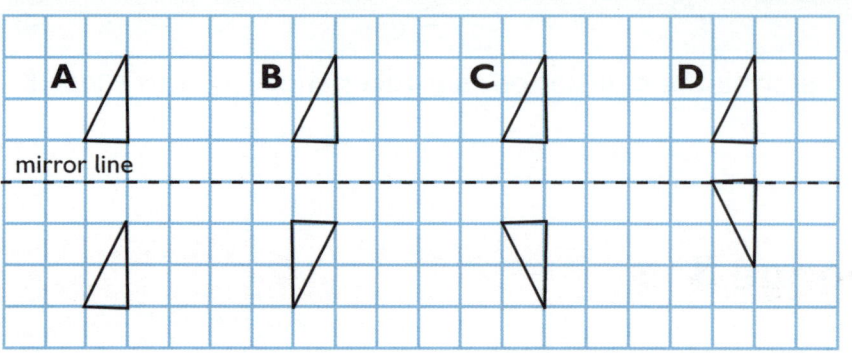

1 mark

2. Draw the reflection of this triangle in the mirror line.
   Use a ruler.

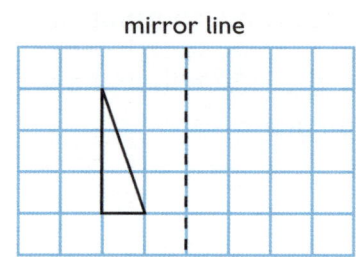

1 mark

3. Draw the reflection of this triangle in the mirror line.
   Use a ruler.

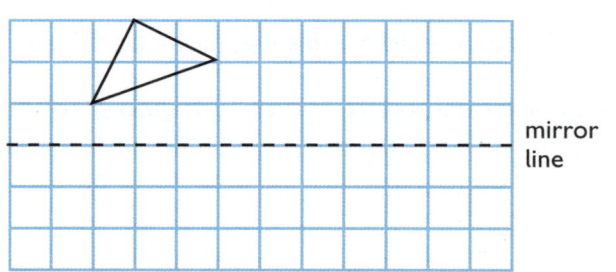

1 mark

Challenge 2

1. Draw the reflection of this rhombus in the mirror line.
   Use a ruler.

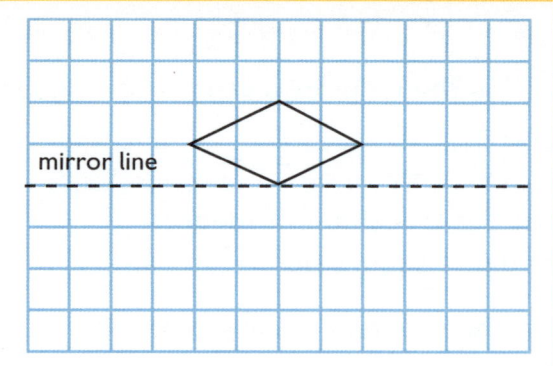

1 mark

2. Draw the reflection of this shape in the mirror line.
   Use a ruler.

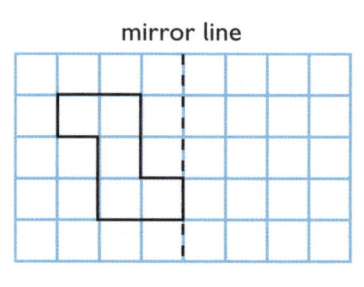

1 mark

98

3. Here is a shape and its reflection.
Draw the mirror line for this reflection.

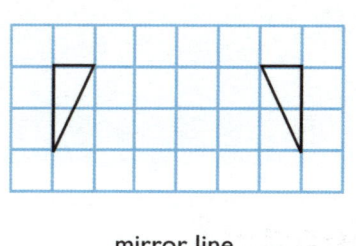

1 mark

4. Draw the reflection of this shape in the mirror line.
Use a ruler.

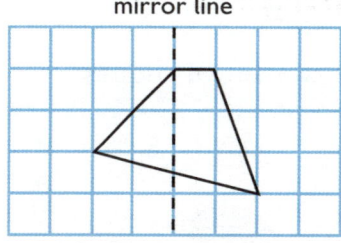

1 mark

Challenge 3

1. Draw the reflection of this shape in the mirror line.
Use a ruler.

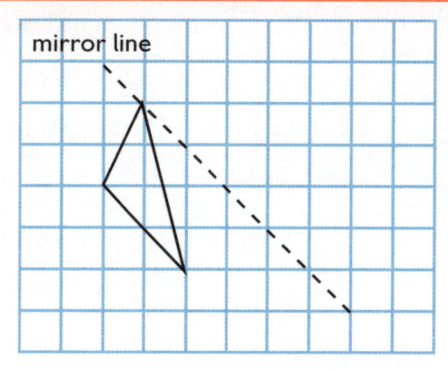

1 mark

2. Draw the reflection of this rectangle in the mirror line.
Use a ruler.

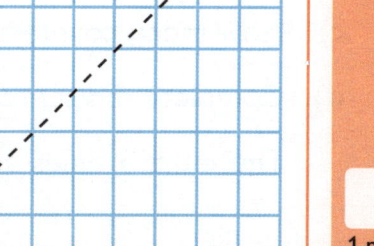

1 mark

3. a) Draw the reflection of this shape in the vertical mirror line.

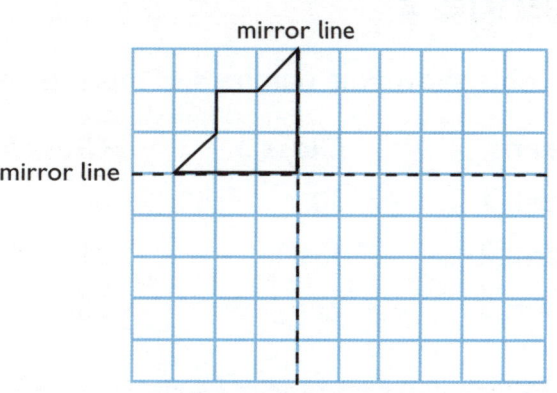

b) Draw the reflection of the whole shape in the horizontal mirror line.

c) Write down the number of lines of symmetry in the final shape. ....

3 marks

How am I doing?   Total marks: ___ / 12

Geometry – properties of shapes

Tables

Challenge 1

1. Here is a set of shapes:

   Complete this table for these shapes.

Shape	Number of shapes
Triangle	
Quadrilateral	
Pentagon	

   3 marks

2. Drina has a box of counters. She records the colours of the counters in a table.

Colour	Number of counters
Red	15
Blue	12
Green	10
Yellow	4
White	5

   a) How many of the counters are green? ....

   b) How many of the counters are either red or white? ....

   c) How many counters are there in total? ....

   d) Complete this sentence:

   There are 3 times as many blue counters as .... counters.

   4 marks

Challenge 2

1. The table shows the numbers of merit points for four classes over 3 terms.

Term	Class 3	Class 4	Class 5	Class 6
Term 1	30	40	16	36
Term 2	15	21	18	24
Term 3	27	26	25	11

   a) Which class had most merit points for Term 3? ....

   b) What is the difference between the highest and lowest numbers of merit points in Term 2? ....

   c) Which class had the most merit points, in total? ....

   d) Which class had the fewest merit points, in total? ....

   4 marks

2. Layla records the numbers of birds in her garden at different times during the day.

She makes a tally mark (|) for each bird she sees.

She groups the tally marks in 5s, like this: ||||

The table shows some of her results.

Time interval	Number of birds
9.00 to 9.05 am	||||
11.00 to 11.05 am	||||	
1.00 to 1.05 pm	|||| ||||
3.00 to 3.05 pm	
4.00 to 4.05 pm	

a) From 3.00 to 3.05 pm there were 8 birds. Draw tally marks in the table to show this.

b) From 4.00 to 4.05 pm there were half as many birds as there were from 11.00 to 11.05 am.

Draw tally marks in the table to show this.

c) In which time interval did Layla record the most birds?

....

3 marks

Challenge 3

1. The table shows the animals a vet saw one day.

The vet saw 20 animals in total. He saw equal numbers of guinea pigs and parrots.

He saw twice as many rabbits as parrots.

Write the numbers of guinea pigs, parrots and rabbits in the table.

Animal	Number
Cat	7
Dog	5
Guinea pig	
Parrot	
Rabbit	

3 marks

2. This table shows the numbers of children who do drama and athletics on different days.

	Monday	Wednesday	Friday
Drama	54	48	32
Athletics	63	35	56

a) How many more children do drama than athletics on Wednesday? ....

b) Which is the most popular day for drama? ....

c) Which is most popular on Fridays – drama or athletics? ....

3 marks

How am I doing?   Total marks: ☐ /20

Statistics

Timetables

Challenge 1

1. The table shows the sunrise and sunset times one day in two cities, Paris and Marseille.

	Sunrise	Sunset
Paris	8.21 am	6.49 pm
Marseille	8 am	6.45 pm

   a) Which city had the earliest sunrise? ....

   b) How much later was sunset in Paris than in Marseille? ....

   c) Which city had the longest time between sunrise and sunset? ....

   d) Complete this sentence:

   In Paris, sunset was .... hours .... minutes after sunrise.

   4 marks

Challenge 2

1. Here is part of a bus timetable from the bus station to the hospital.

Bus station	07:12	07:55	08:40	09:07
High Street	07:19	08:02	08:47	09:14
Railway station	07:24	08:07	08:52	09:19
London Road	07:33	08:16	09:01	09:28
Hospital	07:45	08:28	09:13	09:40

   a) Maisy catches the bus at the railway station at 08:07.

   What time does she arrive at the hospital? ....

   b) How long does the bus journey from the bus station to the hospital take? ....

   c) Sid arrives at the High Street at half past 8.

   How long does he have to wait until the next bus to the hospital? ....

   d) Amol needs to be at the hospital by 9 o'clock.

   What time is the latest bus he can catch from the bus station? ....

   4 marks

102

Challenge 3

1. Here is a train timetable from Tomson Green to Buckler's Halt.

	Train 1	Train 2	Train 3	Train 4
Tomson Green	14:41	16:27	19:12	21:36
Kingsbury	15:05	16:51	19:36	22:00
Clapton	15:13	16:59	-----	22:08
Medford	15:29	----	19:56	22:24
Buckler's Halt	15:55	17:34	20:22	22:50

a) Which train does not stop at Medford? ....

b) How long does the train journey from Tomson Green to Kingsbury take?  ....

c) Which train takes the shortest time to travel from Tomson Green to Buckler's Halt? ....

d) Train 1 arrives 13 minutes late in Medford.

What time does it arrive in Medford? ....

e) Ranjit is in Clapton and wants to arrive in Buckler's Halt before 6 pm.

What time is the latest train he can catch from Clapton? ....

5 marks

2. The timetable shows Kai's lessons one week.

	9am	10am	11am	11.15am	12.30pm	1pm	2pm	3pm
Monday	Maths	Science	Break	PE	Lunch break	English	Art	School ends
Tuesday	English	Maths	Break	Drama	Lunch break	History	Pottery	School ends
Wednesday	PE	English	Break	Maths	Lunch break	Science	Geography	School ends
Thursday	English	ICT	Break	Swimming	Lunch break	Maths	RS	School ends
Friday	Science	Music	Break	English	Lunch break	Maths	PE	School ends

a) What lesson does Kai have at 1pm on Thursday? ....

b) How many PE lessons does Kai have in one week? ....

c) How long is the lunch break? ....

d) How long is the swimming lesson? ....

e) Which subjects does Kai have every day? ....

f) How many hours of Maths does Kai have every week? ....

6 marks

How am I doing?   **Total marks:** ..../19

Statistics 103

Bar charts and pictograms

Challenge 1

1. Laurie asked people to choose their favourite fruit. The table shows his results.

Fruit	Number of people
Banana	14
Pineapple	3
Mango	10
Grapes	5

Complete this bar chart for Laurie's data.

Favourite fruit

3 marks

2. The pictogram shows the numbers of sandwiches a café sells on different days.

Sandwiches sold

Mon	⊠ ⊠ ⊠ ⊠
Tues	⊠ ⊠ ⊠ ⊠ ▽
Weds	⊠ ⊠ ⊠ ▽
Thurs	⊠ ⊠ ⊠ ⊠ ⊠ ▽
Fri	

Key
⊠ = 4 sandwiches

a) How many sandwiches did the café sell on Wednesday? ....

b) On Friday the café sold half as many sandwiches as they did on Tuesday.

   Draw symbols in the pictogram to show this.

2 marks

Challenge 2

1 Sophie counted the numbers of pictures in the books in the classroom. The bar chart shows her results.

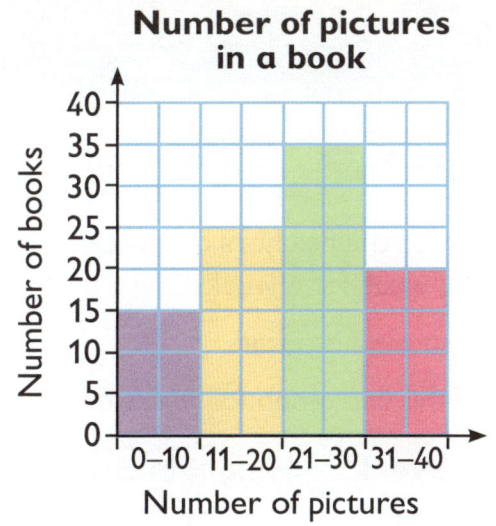

a) How many books had fewer than 21 pictures? ....

b) How many books had more than 10 pictures? ....

c) How many books are represented in the bar chart? ....

3 marks

Challenge 3

1 The bar chart shows the numbers of people on different rides in a theme park.

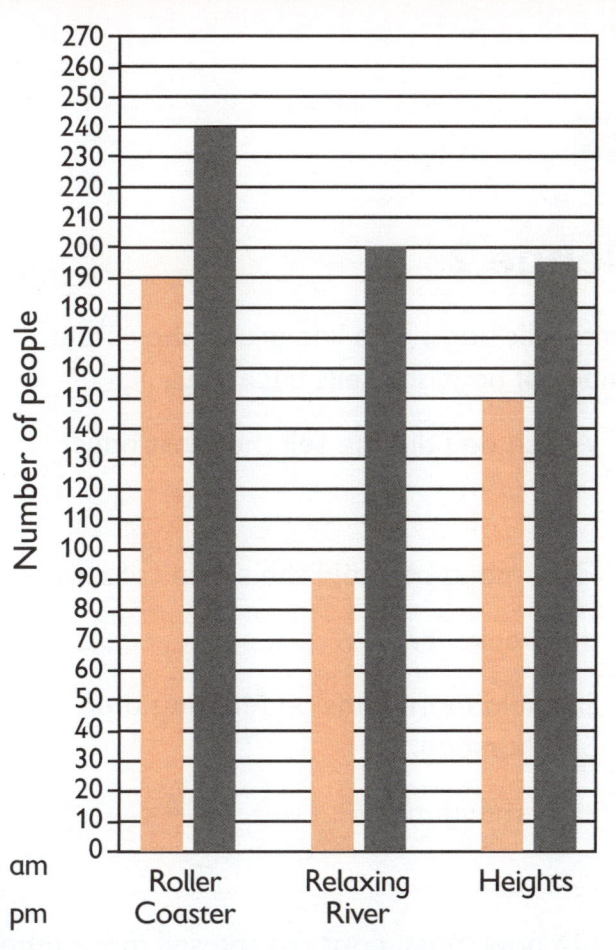

a) Which ride was most popular in the morning?

....

b) Which ride was least popular in the afternoon?

....

c) Which ride had fewest people in the whole day?

....

d) How many more people went on the Relaxing River ride in the afternoon than in the morning?

....

4 marks

How am I doing?   Total marks: ☐ / 12

Statistics

Line graphs

Challenge 1

1. Jake recorded the height of a sunflower plant every week for 6 weeks.

   The table shows his results.

   Complete this line graph for Jake's data.

Week	Height in cm
1	20
2	35
3	45
4	60
5	70
6	85

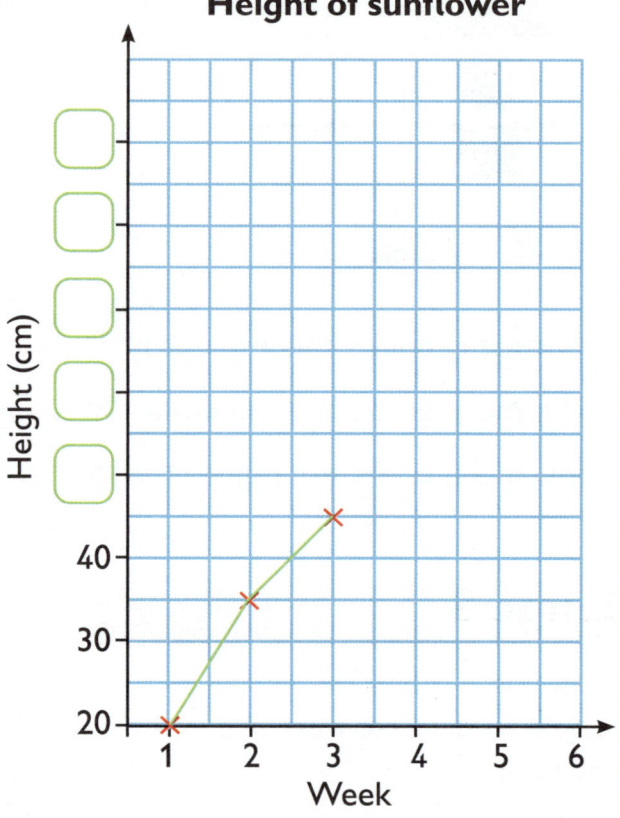

4 marks

Challenge 2

1. Vashti sells bags. This line graph shows the number of bags she sells each day.

   a) Which day did she sell the most bags?

   ....

   b) How many bags did she sell in total at the weekend? ....

   c) She sold more bags on Monday than on Thursday.

   How many more?

   ....

   d) On how many days did she sell more than 15 bags?

   ....

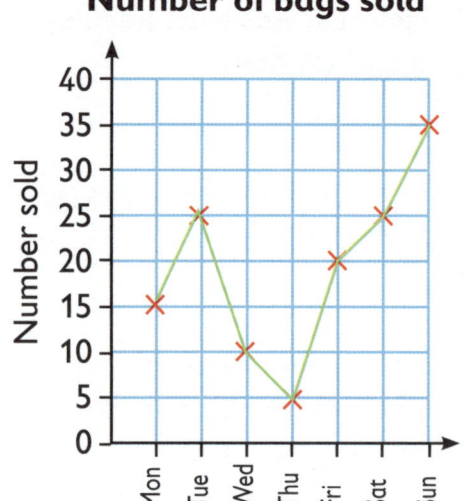

4 marks

Challenge 3

1. This graph shows the outdoor temperature one day in January.

   a) Between which two times did the temperature remain the same?

   Between .... and ....

   b) Between which two times was the temperature increasing?

   Between .... and ....

   c) Between which two times was the temperature decreasing?

   Between .... and ....

   d) What was the temperature at 12 o'clock? ....

   e) For how many hours was the temperature 0°C or above? ....

   5 marks

2. Manjit hits a ball. The graph shows the height of the ball at different times.

   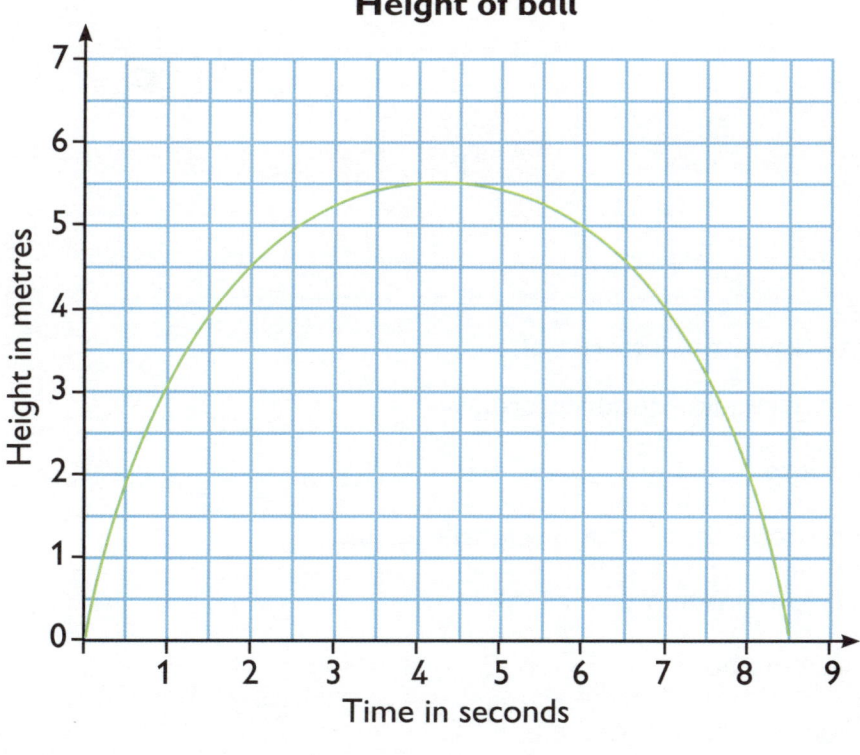

   a) For how many seconds is the ball at a height of 2 metres or more? ....

   b) Estimate the maximum height that the ball reached. ....

   c) At which two times was the ball at a height of 4.5 metres? .... and ....

   4 marks

How am I doing?   Total marks: ☐ /17

Statistics

Progress test 4

1. Draw an obtuse angle.
   Use a ruler.

2. Draw a line at an angle of 30° to this line.

   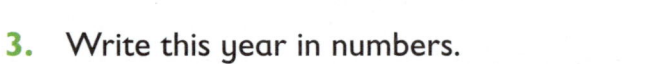

3. Write this year in numbers.
   MDLXXX ....

4. Here are some shapes drawn on a squared grid.

   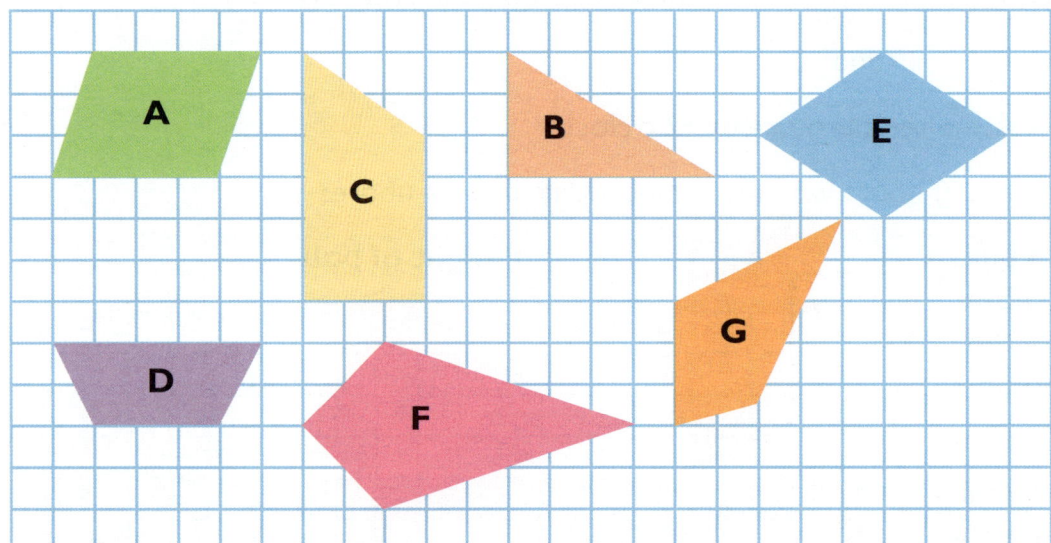

   Write down the letter(s) of:

   a) an irregular quadrilateral. ....

   b) a kite. ....

   c) a shape that is not a quadrilateral. ....

   d) two trapeziums. ....

   e) a rhombus. ....

5. At 9 am the temperature is −2°C.
   At 1 pm the temperature is 6°C.
   How many degrees does the temperature rise between 9 am and 1 pm?

   ....°C

6. Work out the volume of this cuboid, made from 1 cm³ cubes.

.... cm³   1 mark

7. Work out:

   a) $\frac{3}{5}$ of 20 = ...   b) $3 \times 1\frac{1}{2}$ = ...   2 marks

8. What is the acute angle between the hands on this clock?

.... °   1 mark

9. Here is a diagram of a rectangular field.

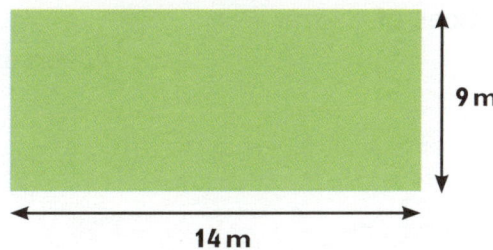

9 m

14 m

   a) Work out the perimeter of the field.

.... m

   b) Work out the area of the field.

.... m²   2 marks

10. Tick (✓) all the regular polygons.

   a) 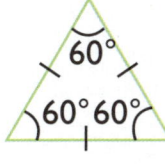   b)    c)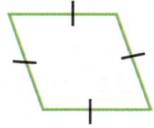

   d)    e) 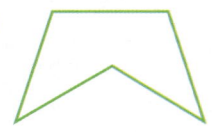   f)

   2 marks

Progress test 4   109

11. Here are some words used to describe triangles.

| acute   obtuse   right-angled   scalene   isosceles |

Use two of the words in the box to describe this triangle.

....

2 marks

12. Calculate the size of the reflex angle in this diagram.

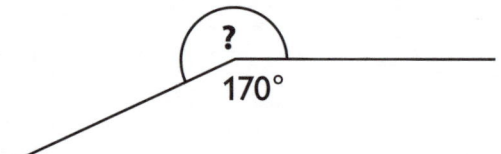

....

1 mark

13. These coordinates are three vertices of a kite.

(2, 4)   (4, 0)   (4, 6)

A vertex is a corner.

a) Plot the points on the grid.

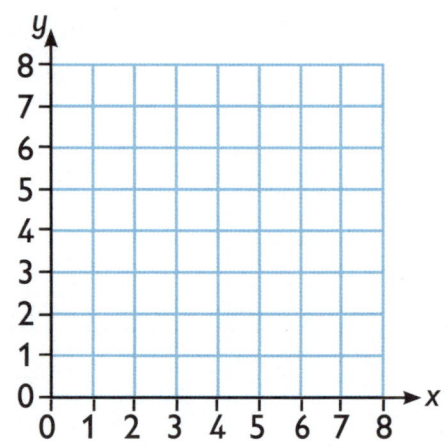

1 mark

b) What are the coordinates of the fourth vertex?   (................, ...)

2 marks

14. Write these in order, from smallest to largest.

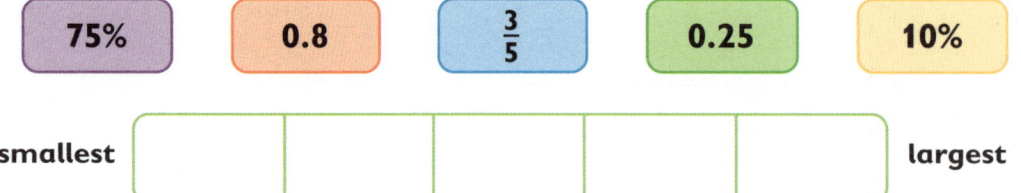

smallest [   ][   ][   ][   ][   ] largest

2 marks

110

15. Here is a train timetable.

	Train 1	Train 2	Train 3
Sopley Bridge	08:45	12:27	17:26
Dramford Lane	09:25	13:25	18:00
Calshott	10:02	14:06	18:24
Inkley Town	10:56	14:42	19:37
Travett Centre	11:29	15:16	19:58
Somersby	12:24	16:03	20:35

Sophie lives in Calshott.

She wants to go to Somersby.

She needs to arrive in Somersby between 3 pm and 5 pm.

What time train should she catch from Calshott? .... 1 mark

16. Four equal angles make a straight line.

What is the size of **one** of these angles? .... 1 mark

17. The line graph shows the numbers of customers at a barber's one week.

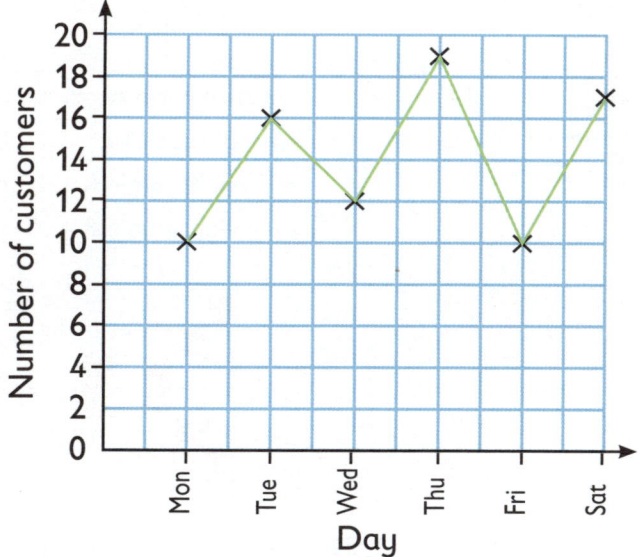

a) Which day had the most customers? ....

b) How many customers were there on Wednesday? ....

c) There were more customers on Saturday than on Friday.

How many more? ....

3 marks

How am I doing?   Total marks: / 30

Answers

For questions worth 1 mark with several answer spaces, all answers should be correct to achieve the mark, unless otherwise indicated.

Pages 4–11 Starter test

1. 28, 35, 42
2. 10.00, 10.06, 10.24, 10.39, 10.42
   [2 marks if all correct, 1 mark if one incorrect]
3. a) 6023   b) 8460   c) 9638   d) 2219
4. 8500
5. 12 squares shaded
6. £4.76
7. 42 cm²
8. a) 15   b) 39   c) 90   d) 54
9. a) two thousand, four hundred and sixty-eight
   b) 1017
10. 24 cm
11. a) 10 000   b) 28 900   c) 19 371   d) 100 000
12. a)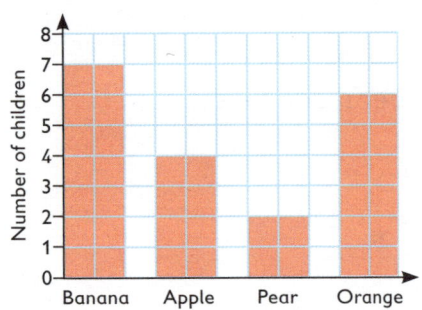
    b) 19
    c) 5
13. a) (3, 2)
    b) and c)
    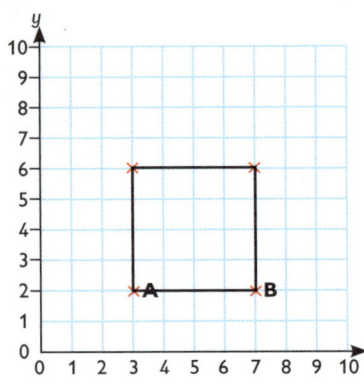
14. $\frac{7}{10} = 0.7$ $\frac{1}{2} = 0.5$ $\frac{1}{4} = 0.25$ $\frac{3}{100} = 0.03$ $\frac{3}{4} = 0.75$
    [2 marks if all correct, 1 mark if one incorrect]
15. 1000
16. 7.45 pm
17. a) parallelogram   b) rectangle
    c) rhombus   d) square
    e) trapezium   f) kite
18. a)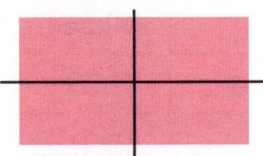
    [1 mark, no marks if diagonal lines are drawn]
    b)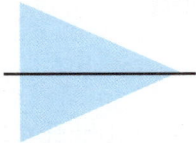
    [1 mark, no marks if incorrect lines are drawn]
    c)
    [1 mark, no marks if incorrect lines are drawn]
    d)
    [1 mark, no marks if incorrect lines are drawn]
19. a) obtuse O   b) acute A
    c) right angle R   d) obtuse O
    e) right angle R   f) acute A
20.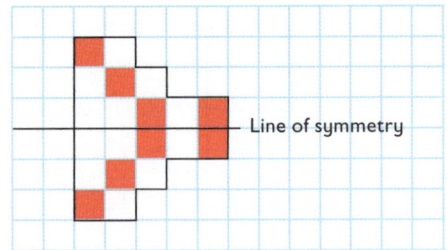
21. a) 5 pm   b) 17:00
22. a) 60   b) 7   c) 1
    d) 1   e) 60   f) 31
23. 3 squares left and 4 squares up
24. a) −5   b) −3   c) 1   d) 4
25. a) 3765   b) 890
26. a) 48   b) 8   c) 9   d) 121
27. 1281
28. 5.20, 5.18, 5.16
29. a) $\frac{5}{6}$ b) $\frac{4}{9}$ c) $\frac{6}{7}$ d) $\frac{2}{5}$

30. a) 6   b) 14

Pages 12–13
Challenge 1
1. 840, 3840, 4840
2. a) fourteen thousand, two hundred and eighty-seven
   b) 20 000
   c) 1 000 000
3. 70 047, 74 740, 407 006, 407 020, 470 000
   [2 marks if all correct, 1 if only one incorrect]

Challenge 2
1. a) 203 601   b) 600 530
2. Lily's
3. a) and b)

Challenge 3
1. a) 79 497   b) 79 506   c) 79 596
   d) 80 496   e) 89 496   f) 179 496
2.

Number	100 000 more than the number
563 000	663 000
970 251	1 070 251
1 036 050	1 136 050
1 900 000	2 million

3. a) 48 900   b) 489   c) 4890
4. a) 120   b) 1200   c) 12 000   d) 1 200 000
5. 12 100

Pages 14–15
Challenge 1
1. a) 7000   b) 27 000   c) 19 000
   d) 329 000   e) 743 000   f) 38 000
2. a) 9842, 9835   b) 9860, 9926
   c) 9842, 9926, 9860, 9835, 10 312
   [2 marks for all 5 numbers, 1 mark if 1 or 2 are missing]

Challenge 2
1. a) 80 000   b) 30 000   c) 190 000
   d) 290 000   e) 280 000   f) 560 000
2. a) 300 000   b) 300 000   c) 100 000
   d) 500 000   e) 900 000   f) 700 000
3. 74 000
4. 180 000

Challenge 3
1. 1 000 000
2. a) 34 999   b) 25 000
3. b) 8000 ÷ 2000 = 4
   c) 80 000 ÷ 20 000 = 5
4. b) 400   c) 40
   d) 50 000   e) 300 000   f) 500 000
5. a) 4000, 60 000
   b) 64 000

Pages 16–17
Challenge 1
1. a) 5   b) 1   c) 10   d) 100   e) 50
2. 12
3. XXVII   XXXIII   XLIX   LXXIV   XC
   [2 marks if all correct, 1 mark if one incorrect]
4. a) LXVI = 66   b) XCIV = 94

Challenge 2
1. a) 500   b) 1000
2. 606
3. 1645
4. 1533

Challenge 3
1. a) 24   b) 30   c) 31   d) 75
   e) 185   f) 230   g) 405   h) 100
2. 1936
3. CXL, CC, CCXX
4. 2012

Pages 18–19
Challenge 1
1.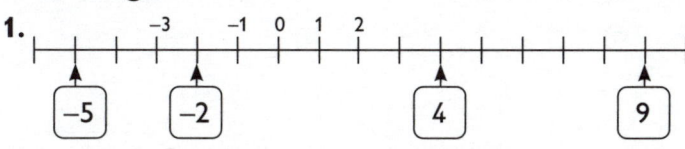
2. a) 0°C   b) 7°C   c) −2°C
3. a) 6°C   b) −4°C   c) −5°C   d) −18°C

Challenge 2
1. −10°C   −8°C   −4°C   0°C   8°C   13°C
   [2 marks if all correct, 1 mark if one incorrect]
2. 27°C   9°C   3°C   −1°C   −18°C   −19°C
   [2 marks if all correct, 1 mark if one incorrect]
3. −3°C
4. 4°C
5. −5°C

Challenge 3
1. 5°C
2. 3°C
3. a) 0   b) 5   c) 4th
4. 5 degrees

Answers 113

Pages 20–21
Challenge 1
1. 9, 18, 27, 36
2. 1, 2, 4, 8
3. a) 25   b) 100   c) 1   d) 36
4. 2, 3, 5, 7, 11   [2 marks if all correct, 1 mark if one incorrect or missing]

Challenge 2
1. a) 1   b) 8   c) 27   d) 1000
2. Any four from: 7, 21, 35, 49, 63, 77, 91   [2 marks if all correct, 1 mark if one incorrect]
3. 1, 3
4. 1, 2, 4   [2 marks if all correct, 1 mark if one incorrect or missing]
5. 1, 4, 9, 16   [2 marks if all correct, 1 mark if one incorrect]
6. 11, 13, 17, 19, 23, 29   [2 marks if all correct, 1 mark if one incorrect]
7. a) 7   b) 9   c) 4, 8

Challenge 3
1. 16
2. a) 11   b) 97
3. 9 and 16
4. a) 100   b) 9   c) 16   d) 900
5. a) 54   b) 24   c) 44   d) 1064
6. a) 1, 8, 27, 64, 125   [2 marks if all correct, 1 mark if one incorrect or missing]
   b) 1 and 64
7. a) 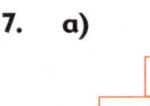   b)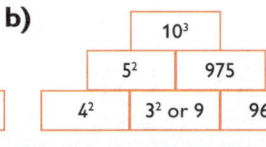

Pages 22–23
Challenge 1
1. a) 14 500   b) 400 000   c) 53 500   d) 103 960
2. a) 6988   b) 58 961   c) 101 258   d) 579 369
3. a)

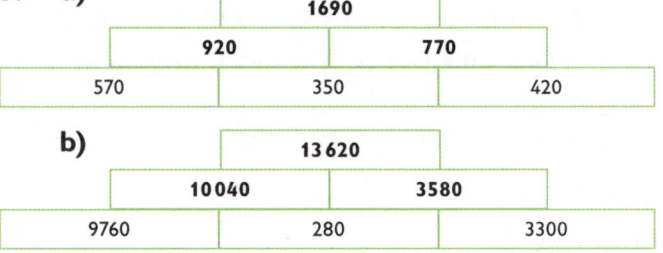

   b)

Challenge 2
1. a) 35 850   b) 515 595   c) 458 900   d) 135 485
2. a) 1350, 650
   b) 45 325, 54 675
3. 734 378
4. Maximum possible answer 18 395, e.g. by adding 9753 + 8642, or 9643 + 8752
   [2 marks for 18 395, 1 mark for a correct calculation with a different total]

Challenge 3
1. a) Max   b) Friday

Pages 24–25
Challenge 1
1. a) 7610   b) 17 000   c) 30 450   d) 301 100
2. a) 6131   b) 44 208   c) 92 915   d) 226 650

Challenge 2
1. a) 15 285   b) 574 625
2. a) 21 025   b) 29 620   c) 55 546   d) 66 401
3. 32 541
4. a)

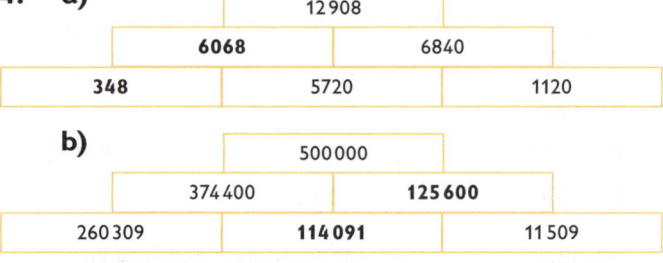

   b)

5. a) 12 785   b) 56 980   c) 84 215   d) 124 687
6. 80 344

Challenge 3
1. a) 5423   b) 8989   c) 17 022   d) 23 841
2. £14 165

Pages 26–27
Challenge 1
1. a) 60   b) 72   c) 42
   d) 132   e) 63   f) 48
2. a) 29 700   b) 518 000   c) 350 700
   d) 472 000   e) 462 150   f) 250 000
3. a) 378   b) 1248   c) 516   d) 4216

Challenge 2
1. a) 36   b) 1600   c) 216   d) 36 000
2. a) 7182   b) 4590   c) 64 476   d) 212 313
3. 8760

Challenge 3
1. 21 440 km
2. a) 2840   b) 363 900   c) 848 000   d) 1 120 000
3. 2 × 3 × 5 × 7 × 11 = 2310
   [2 marks: 1 mark for correct prime numbers, 1 mark for correct answer]
4. 9072

Pages 28–29

Challenge 1
1. a) 6 b) 6 c) 12 d) 11 e) 8 f) 5
2. a) 256 b) 950 c) 2531 d) 500 e) 3420 f) 1000
3. a) 42 b) 36 c) 1223 d) 125
4. 18

Challenge 2
1. a) 123 b) 384 c) 781 d) 525
2. a) 58 b) 2
3. 16
4. 30

Challenge 3
1. a) 1537 remainder 3 b) 333 remainder 3 c) 416 remainder 8 d) 247 remainder 3
2. a) 682 b) 463
3. a) Yes, 1062 ÷ 9 = 118
   b) No, 1850 ÷ 12 = 154 remainder 2

Pages 30–31

Challenge 1
1. 175
2. 700
3. 124
4. £519

Challenge 2
1. a) 4 hours 30 minutes
   b) 13 hours 30 minutes
2. 2.5 bananas, 250 g strawberries, 10 scoops ice cream, 1250 ml milk
3. £13

Challenge 3
1. Niall 82, Lissa 105
2. a) 64 b) 284

Progress test 1

Pages 32–35
1. 40 000
2. five hundred and thirty-two thousand, four hundred and ten
3. 12, 24, 36, 48
4. a) 7 b) 7 c) 12 d) 11
5. a) 100 b) 1000
6. 111 202
7. a) 1, 2, 4, 5, 10, 20 b) 2, 5
8. a) 200 000 b) 10 000
9. 434 779
10. −6°C   −4°C   −2°C   0°C   3°C   5°C
    [2 marks if all correct, 1 mark if one incorrect]
11. 14 910
12. 28 926
13.

1000 less than the number	Number	100 000 more than the number
26 000	27 000	127 000
248 000	249 000	349 000
899 000	900 000	1 million

14. 81 460
15. 35 200
16. 119 000
17. 4°C
18. 1380
19. 2008
20. 148
21. 110 000
22. 1, 2, 4
23. £243 781
24. a) 48 000 b) 6000 c) 54 000
25. a) 3602 b) 536 c) 9990
26. Blue whale, 116 500 kg
27. 1936
28. 1 + 2 + 3 + 4 + 6 + 12 = 28
29. 1, 8, 27
30. a) 1064 b) 65
31. 67 597 000

Pages 36–37

Challenge 1
1. a) $\frac{1}{4}$ b) $\frac{3}{4}$
2. $\frac{2}{4}$ $\frac{1}{2}$
3. $\frac{3}{6}$ $\frac{1}{2}$
4.

[1 mark for both correct, with no extra diagrams ticked]

Challenge 2
1. Any 6 squares shaded
2. a) 2 out of 8 squares shaded, 3 out of 12 squares shaded.
   b) $\frac{2}{8}$ and $\frac{3}{12}$ [2 marks: accept any other fractions that are equivalent to $\frac{1}{4}$]
3. a) 7 b) 20
4. $\frac{4}{8}$ $\frac{9}{18}$ [1 mark for both correct, with no extra fractions circled]

Challenge 3

1. $\frac{1}{5}$
2. a) $\frac{2}{6}$ b) $\frac{3}{6}$
3. Any 8 squares shaded
4. a) $\frac{50}{100}$ b) $\frac{25}{100}$ c) $\frac{75}{100}$
5. a) $\frac{2}{12}$ b) $\frac{3}{12}$ c) $\frac{4}{12}$
   d) $\frac{6}{12}$ e) $\frac{8}{12}$ f) $\frac{9}{12}$

Pages 38–39

Challenge 1

1. b) $\frac{5}{4}$ $1\frac{1}{4}$
   c) $\frac{13}{5}$ $2\frac{3}{5}$
   d) $\frac{5}{3}$ $1\frac{2}{3}$

2. a) $\frac{7}{4}$ $\frac{11}{6}$ $\frac{9}{5}$
   [1 mark for all three correct, with no extra values circled]
   b) $1\frac{3}{8}$ $2\frac{1}{5}$ $3\frac{1}{7}$
   [1 mark for all three correct, with no extra values ticked]

Challenge 2

1. $\frac{7}{3}$ $1\frac{4}{5}$ $\frac{11}{9}$ $3\frac{1}{4}$ $\frac{12}{5}$
   [1 mark for all five correct, with no extra values circled]

2. 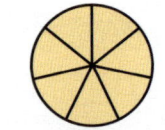 $1\frac{4}{7}$

3. 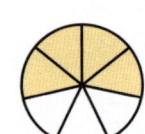 $2\frac{7}{10}$

4. b) $1\frac{3}{4}$ $\frac{7}{4}$
   c) $1\frac{2}{5}$ $\frac{7}{5}$

Challenge 3

1. b) $1\frac{1}{4}$ c) $2\frac{1}{5}$
2. $4\frac{3}{5} = \frac{23}{5}$ $8\frac{1}{10} = \frac{81}{10}$ $\frac{7}{3} = 2\frac{1}{3}$ $\frac{9}{2} = 4\frac{1}{2}$
   $6\frac{4}{5} = \frac{34}{5}$ $\frac{11}{4} = 2\frac{3}{4}$ $\frac{29}{9} = 3\frac{2}{9}$

Pages 40–41

Challenge 1

1. $\frac{1}{10}$ $\frac{1}{6}$ $\frac{1}{5}$ $\frac{1}{4}$ $\frac{1}{3}$ $\frac{1}{2}$
   [2 marks if all correct, 1 mark if one incorrect]
2. a) <   b) <   c) <   d) >

Challenge 2

1. a) >   b) >   c) >
2. $\frac{1}{100}$ $\frac{1}{10}$ $\frac{3}{10}$ $\frac{41}{100}$ $\frac{87}{100}$ $\frac{9}{10}$
   [2 marks if all correct, 1 mark if one incorrect]
3. $\frac{7}{8}$ $\frac{3}{4}$ $\frac{5}{8}$ $\frac{9}{16}$ $\frac{1}{2}$ $\frac{1}{4}$
   [2 marks if all correct, 1 mark if one incorrect]
4. a) $\frac{2}{5}$ b) $\frac{7}{8}$ c) $\frac{6}{8}$ d) $\frac{2}{5}$
5. a) any number greater than 1
   b) 3, 2 or 1
   c) 8, or any number greater than 8
   d) 6, or any positive number less than 6

Challenge 3

1. $2\frac{2}{3}$ $2\frac{5}{8}$ $2\frac{3}{4}$ $2\frac{5}{6}$ $3\frac{7}{10}$ $3\frac{4}{5}$
   [2 marks if all correct, 1 mark if one incorrect]
2. $\frac{2}{3}$ $\frac{5}{3}$ $2\frac{1}{3}$ $2\frac{2}{3}$ $\frac{9}{3}$ $3\frac{1}{3}$
   [2 marks if all correct, 1 mark if one incorrect]
3. $\frac{8}{12}$
4. $\frac{7}{12}$

Pages 42–43

Challenge 1

1. a) $\frac{3}{4}$ b) $\frac{3}{5}$ c) $\frac{3}{8}$
   d) $\frac{4}{15}$ e) $\frac{51}{100}$ f) $\frac{7}{20}$
2. a) $\frac{3}{4}$ b) $\frac{4}{5}$ c) $\frac{5}{7}$ d) $\frac{3}{10}$
3. $\frac{1}{3}$

Challenge 2

1. a) $\frac{3}{8}$ b) $\frac{3}{10}$ c) $\frac{3}{8}$
   d) $\frac{5}{10}$ (or $\frac{1}{2}$)   e) $\frac{5}{8}$ f) $\frac{13}{100}$
2. a) $\frac{9}{8}$ b) $\frac{11}{10}$ c) $\frac{17}{10}$ d) $\frac{9}{6}$
3. $\frac{1}{8}$
4. No

Challenge 3

1. a) $\frac{5}{8}$ b) $\frac{5}{8}$ c) $\frac{44}{100}$ (or $\frac{11}{25}$)   d) $\frac{3}{12}$ (or $\frac{1}{4}$)
2. a) $1\frac{1}{4}$ b) $1\frac{3}{10}$ c) $2\frac{1}{4}$ d) $1\frac{5}{6}$
3. $\frac{3}{8}$ of a litre
4. $\frac{1}{4}$ and $\frac{3}{6}$
5.

Fraction	Fraction + $\frac{1}{2}$
$\frac{1}{8}$	$\frac{5}{8}$
$\frac{5}{12}$	$\frac{11}{12}$
$\frac{6}{14}$	$\frac{13}{14}$
$\frac{7}{20}$	$\frac{17}{20}$
$\frac{1}{16}$	$\frac{9}{16}$

Pages 44–45

Challenge 1
1. a) $\frac{3}{4}$ b) $\frac{4}{5}$ c) $\frac{5}{8}$ d) $\frac{8}{9}$
2. a) $\frac{18}{100}$ (or $\frac{9}{50}$) b) $\frac{63}{100}$
   c) $\frac{60}{100}$ (or $\frac{6}{10}$ or $\frac{3}{5}$) d) $\frac{66}{100}$ (or $\frac{33}{50}$)

Challenge 2
1. a) 3 b) 3 c) 15 d) 9
2. a) 5 b) $7\frac{1}{2}$ c) 10 d) $12\frac{1}{2}$
3. a) $3\frac{1}{3}$ b) 5 c) $6\frac{2}{3}$ d) $8\frac{1}{3}$

Challenge 3
1. a) $\frac{21}{1000}$ b) $\frac{108}{1000}$ (or $\frac{54}{500}$ or equivalent)
   c) $\frac{606}{1000}$ (or $\frac{303}{500}$) d) $\frac{333}{1000}$
2. b) $\frac{15}{8} = 1\frac{7}{8}$ c) $\frac{9}{4} = 2\frac{1}{4}$ d) $\frac{40}{7} = 5\frac{5}{7}$
   e) $\frac{50}{8} = 6\frac{2}{8}$ (or $6\frac{1}{4}$)
   f) $\frac{130}{100} = 1\frac{30}{100}$ (or $1\frac{3}{10}$)
   g) $\frac{15}{10} = 1\frac{5}{10}$ (or $1\frac{1}{2}$)
   h) $\frac{63}{5} = 12\frac{3}{5}$
3. a) < b) < c) > d) <
4. 14
5. 8

Pages 46–47

Challenge 1
1. $\frac{1}{4} = 0.25$ $\frac{1}{2} = 0.5$ $\frac{3}{4} = 0.75$
2. $\frac{7}{10} = 0.7$ $\frac{7}{100} = 0.07$ $\frac{21}{100} = 0.21$
   $\frac{9}{100} = 0.09$ $\frac{49}{100} = 0.49$

[2 marks if all correct, 1 mark if one incorrect]

Challenge 2
1.

Words	Fraction	Decimal
1 hundredth	$\frac{1}{100}$	0.01
3 hundredths	$\frac{3}{100}$	**0.03**
9 tenths	$\frac{9}{10}$	**0.9**
1 thousandth	$\frac{1}{1000}$	**0.001**
243 thousandths	$\frac{243}{1000}$	0.243
13 hundredths	$\frac{13}{100}$	**0.13**
51 hundredths	$\frac{51}{100}$	0.51
129 thousandths	$\frac{129}{1000}$	0.129
7 thousandths	$\frac{7}{1000}$	**0.007**
301 thousandths	$\frac{301}{1000}$	0.301

[9 marks: 1 mark for each row correct]

2. a) $\frac{1}{10}, \frac{100}{1000}$ b) $\frac{3}{10}, 0.300$
   c) $\frac{7}{10}, 0.70, \frac{70}{1000}$ d) $\frac{25}{100}, \frac{250}{1000}$
   e) $0.09, \frac{90}{1000}$ f) $0.17, 0.170, \frac{170}{1000}$
3. a) 23 b) 4 c) 160
   d) 50 e) 9200 f) 6810

Challenge 3
1. a) > b) < c) > d) > e) > f) <
2. a) 3.5 b) 72.4 c) 0.04
   d) 0.007 e) 8.47 f) 0.081
3. 0.005   0.04   0.17   0.327   0.51   0.6

[2 marks if all correct, 1 mark if one incorrect]

Pages 48–49

Challenge 1
1. a) 6 cm b) 3 cm c) 5 cm
2. a) 5 b) 6 c) 13 d) 9
   e) 23 f) 100 g) 993 h) 1000

Challenge 2
1. a) £2 b) £2 c) £8
   d) £2 e) £1 f) £5
2. £20
3. a) 7 b) 27 c) 103
   d) 5220 e) 39491 f) 932556
4. a) 16.8 b) 29.5 c) 73.6
   d) 283.5 e) 1304.6 f) 2047.8

Challenge 3
1. 9.65
2. a) 6.25 + 5.34 = 11.59
      rounded to 1 decimal place 11.6
   b) 15.31 + 8.42 = 23.73
      rounded to 1 decimal place 23.7
   c) 24.86 − 5.14 = 19.72
      rounded to 1 decimal place 19.7
   d) 75.03 − 10.25 = 64.78
      rounded to 1 decimal place 64.8
   e) 120.46 × 2 = 240.92
      rounded to 1 decimal place 240.9
   f) 525 ÷ 100 = 5.25
      rounded to 1 decimal place 5.3
3. 38 cm

Pages 50–51

Challenge 1
1. a) 10 squares shaded yellow
   b) 25 squares shaded green
   c) 1 square shaded blue
2. $33\% = \frac{33}{100}$ $6\% = \frac{6}{100}$ $90\% = \frac{90}{100}$
   $76\% = \frac{76}{100}$ $9\% = \frac{9}{100}$

[2 marks if all correct, 1 mark if one incorrect]

Challenge 2

1. 54% = 0.54   10% = 0.1   45% = 0.45
   5% = 0.05   1% = 0.01   50% = 0.5
   [2 marks if all correct, 1 mark if one incorrect]
2. a) 25%   b) 50%   c) 20%
   d) 10%   e) 60%   f) 70%

Challenge 3

1. a) 60%   b) $\frac{1}{4}$ c) 0.99
   d) 10%   e) 40%   f) $\frac{3}{4}$
2. $\frac{1}{4}$ 30%   0.4   42% $\frac{11}{25}$
   [2 marks if all correct, 1 mark if one incorrect]
3. a) £10   b) 9 cm   c) 21 grams   d) £3

Pages 52–53

Challenge 1

1. 40%
2. 54
3. 0.05 and 0.1

Challenge 2

1. 4.8 metres
2. a)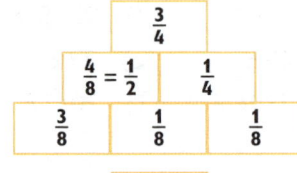

   b)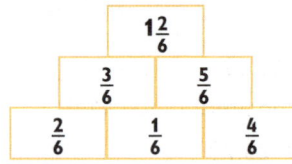

3. a) ÷ 100   b) × 10
4. 9

Challenge 3

1. $\frac{5}{2} + \frac{4}{8} = 3$
2. a) 350   b) 346.6
3. 6

Progress test 2

Pages 54–57

1. 8879
2. $\frac{5}{20}$ $\frac{1}{4}$
3. a) 1, 2, 3, 4, 6, 12   b) 12, 24, 36, 48
4. −4°C
5. $\frac{63}{100}$
6. 65%
7. a) 74 860   b) 74 900
8. $\frac{11}{12}$

9. −27°C   −9°C   −5°C   8°C   13°C   23°C
   [2 marks if all correct, 1 mark if one incorrect]
10. $\frac{4}{5}$
11. 2, 3, 5, 7, 11
    [2 marks if all correct, 1 mark if one incorrect]
12. a) 17   b) 300
13. a)

    b) $2\frac{3}{5}$
14. a) 3   b) 16
15. 30 thousand, or 30 000
16. a) $\frac{9}{10}$ b) $\frac{5}{8}$
17. Any four squares shaded.
18. 35% = 0.35   10% = 0.1   4% = 0.04
    1% = 0.01   40% = 0.4
    [2 marks if all correct, 1 mark if one incorrect]
19. $1\frac{1}{2}$
20. a) 3   b) 60
21. 1997
22. a) 9.5   b) 12.7
23. a) 49   b) 100   c) 8
24. $\frac{3}{8}$ $\frac{1}{2}$ $\frac{7}{12}$ $\frac{3}{4}$ $\frac{11}{12}$
    [2 marks if all correct, 1 mark if one incorrect]
25. 34 272
26. a) 0.25   b) 0.5   c) 0.75
27. a) 6   b) 28
28. 68.8, £69
29. a) $\frac{53}{100}$ b) $\frac{7}{100}$ c) $\frac{829}{1000}$
30. a) 8.3   b) 13.35
31. a) 15 kg   b) £11
32. $\frac{21}{8}$
33. a) $2\frac{2}{5}$ b) $10\frac{2}{3}$
34. a) 72   b) 12
35. 511 113
36. 50 525

Pages 58–59

Challenge 1

1. millimetre, centimetre, metre, kilometre
   [2 marks if all correct, 1 mark if one incorrect]
2. a) 100   b) 10
3. a) 1000   b) 1000   c) 1000
4. a) 400   b) 650   c) 1200   d) 50 000

Challenge 2

1. a) 5   b) 3.5   c) 20   d) 0.45
2. a) 2000   b) 310   c) 5000
   d) 3200   e) 24000   f) 1450
3. a) 7.5   b) 0.8   c) 0.5
   d) 0.6   e) 1.5   f) 3.25
4. 300 ml
5. 990 000 g bag

Challenge 3

1. a) 0.015   b) 0.35   c) 0.025
   d) 0.005   e) 1000   f) 0.04
2. a) <   b) >   c) >   d) >   e) <   f) <
3. 20 g, 0.024 kg, 0.2 kg, 400 g, 2.4 kg
   [2 marks if all correct, 1 mark if one incorrect]
4. a) 8   b) 150 ml

Pages 60–61

Challenge 1

1. 22 cm
2. 20 cm
3. Any one of these rectangles (in any orientation).

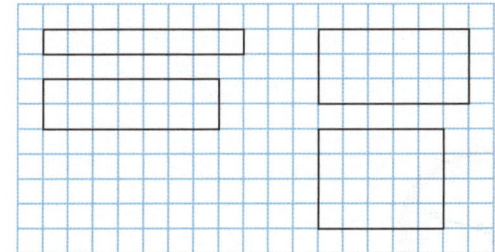

Challenge 2

1. 24 cm
2. 38 cm
3. 128 mm

Challenge 3

1. (Perimeter 52 cm) 6 strips
2. 1.4 m

Pages 62–63

Challenge 1

1. 12 cm²
2. a) 48 cm²   b) 132 cm²   c) 63 cm²

Challenge 2

1. Rectangles can be in any orientation.

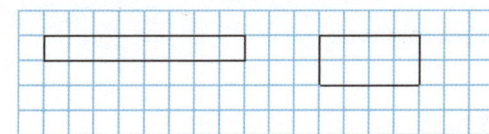

2. 5 cm = 50 mm, 1.6 cm = 16 mm; 800 mm²
3. 48 cm²

Challenge 3

1. 36 cm

2. Area of hall 700 m²
   28 tins of paint
   £420

Pages 64–65

Challenge 1

1. a) 4.38 pm   b) 16:38
2. a) 11.57 am   b) 11:57
3.
4. 60

Challenge 2

1. a) >   b) >   c) <   d) >   e) <   f) <
2. a) Amy   b) 2.31 seconds

Challenge 3

1. 1 hour 17 minutes
2. 7.40 pm or 19:40

Pages 66–67

Challenge 1

1. a) £3.20   b) £5.04
2. £4.20
3. a) £8   b) £3
4. a) £9   b) £6   c) £35
5. £50

Challenge 2

1. £18.50
2. a) £883   b) £8830   c) £883   d) £88.30
3. £25.30
4. a) £240   b) £800

Challenge 3

1. a) £10.75
   b) two adult and two under 2 tickets
   c) £38.95 (1 family ticket, 1 adult ticket, 1 child ticket)
2. £495
3. £1.65

Pages 68–69

Challenge 1

1. a) 8 cm³   b) 8 cm³   c) 8 cm³   d) 11 cm³

Challenge 2

1. a) 16 cm³   b) 72 cm³
2. 4.5 litres
3. 625 ml

Challenge 3

1. a) 27   b) 64

Answers   119

2. Mango 400 ml, Apple 1600 ml

Pages 70–71
Challenge 1
1. 10 cm, 17.5 cm, 25 cm
   6 inches, 8 inches, 11 inches
2. a) 4.4   b) 22   c) 66   d) 220

Challenge 2
1. a) 30   b) 150   c) 75   d) 1800
2.

Weight	Length	Volume or capacity
pound	inch	pint
gram	centimetre	litre
kilogram	kilometre	millilitre
	foot	

3. a) 1140 ml = 1.14(0) litres
   b) 2280 ml = 2.28(0) litres
   c) 5700 ml = 5.7(00) litres

Challenge 3
1. a) Shanice   b) 4.5 cm
2. centimetre, inch, foot, metre
   [2 marks if all correct, 1 mark if one incorrect]
3. a) >   b) <
4. 4.56 litres
5. a) >   b) <

Pages 72–73
Challenge 1
1. 6
2. a) 900 g   b) 250 g   c) 1 teaspoon

Challenge 2
1. 100 g
2. 1152
3. 15

Challenge 3
1. 600
2. £29.40
3. 34.56 litres

Pages 74–75
Challenge 1
1. £4
2. £702
3. 60 ml, 200 ml, $\frac{1}{2}$ litre, $\frac{3}{4}$ litre, 800 ml
   [2 marks if all correct, 1 mark if one incorrect]

Challenge 2
1. a) 9   b) 16.6 m
2. 14 kg

3. 1 pound, 1 kilogram, 5 pounds, 4 kilograms
   [2 marks if all correct, 1 mark if one incorrect]

Challenge 3
1. Shorter side = 12 m
   Perimeter = 56 m
   7 tins, £70
2. a) 28 cm
   b) 9 cm^2

Progress test 3
Pages 76–79
1. 25%
2. 10 136
3. 20:26
4. 1594
5. <
6. a) 4000   b) 500
7. £3.20
8. a) 492.8   b) 490
9. 5 g
10. a) 357 m^2 b) 76 m
11. $4\frac{5}{6}$
12. 28 kg
13. −5°C
14.
15. a) 5   b) 4.3   c) 3000   d) 52
16. £85
17. a) 169   b) 73
18. 12 tins
19. <
20. 1, 2, 3, 6
21. a) $\frac{11}{8}$ b) $\frac{12}{10}$
22. 1, 8
23. 60
24. a) $\frac{7}{8}$ b) $\frac{3}{12}$ or $\frac{1}{4}$
25. 28
26. 6 hours 30 minutes
27. 96 hours 45 minutes
28. £3
29. BC taxis

Pages 80–81

Challenge 1

1.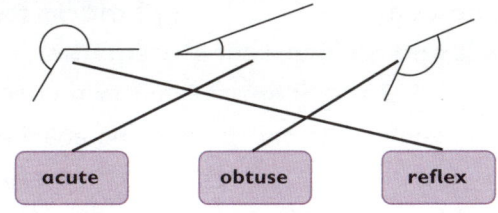
   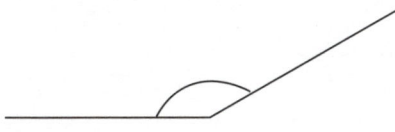

2. a) 40°   b) 55°
3. a) angle b
   b) angle c

Challenge 2

1. 50°
2. Angle of 70° drawn, e.g.

   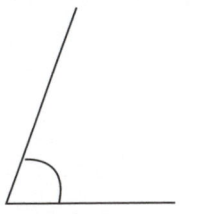

3. Angle of 150° drawn, e.g.

Challenge 3

1. 50° and 30°
2.

Acute	Obtuse	Reflex	Right angle
70°	140°	200°	90°

3. 260°

Pages 82–83

Challenge 1

1. 180°
2. 150°
3. 40°

Challenge 2

1. 80°
2. 205°
3. 360°
4. 60°
5. Angle of 330° drawn, e.g.

   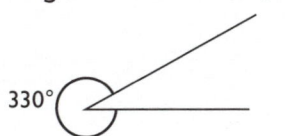

Challenge 3

1. 72°
2. 35°
3. 270°
4. a) 180°   b) 270°   c) window

Pages 84–85

Challenge 1

1.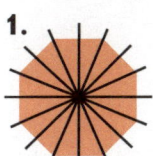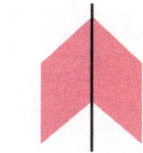

2. a) B and E   b) A and C
   c) D   d) A and B and D

Challenge 2

1.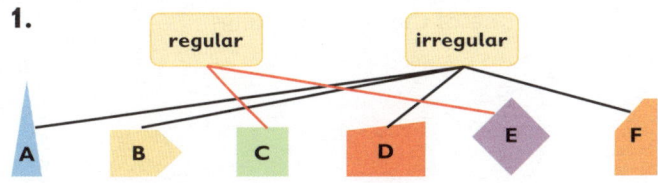

2. Equilateral triangle
3. a) equal   b) equal

Challenge 3

1. The rectangle has all angles equal, but its sides are not all the same length.
2. The hexagon does not have all equal angles, so it is not regular.
3. 8
4. $\frac{7}{8}$

Pages 86–87

Challenge 1

1.

Shape	It is a quadrilateral	It has some parallel sides
	✓	✓
	✗	✓
	✓	✗
	✗	✓
	✗	✗

Challenge 2

1. a) A, C, E   b) B, D   c) E
2. D

Challenge 3

1. Straight lines from two vertices (e.g. A and C, A and E, or B and F or B and D to the centre), e.g.

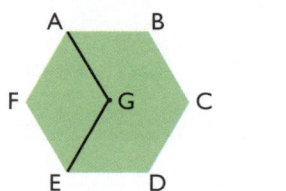 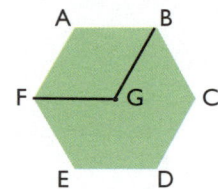

2.  Hexagon

    Heptagon (7 sides)

3. a) Any one of these dashed lines:

   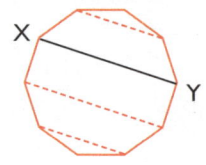

   b) Any one of these dashed lines:

   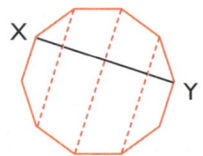

Pages 88–89

Challenge 1
1. D and E
2. a) False   b) True   c) False
   d) True   e) True

Challenge 2
1. 25°
2. 270°
3. 45°

Challenge 3
1. a) 48 cm²
   b) 38 cm
2. a) m = 50°
   b) y = 130°

Pages 90–91

Challenge 1
1.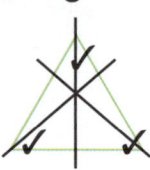

2. right-angled triangles

Challenge 2
1. two equal sides, one obtuse angle, two equal angles, isosceles **[2 marks for all correct and no incorrect statements ticked, 1 mark for at least two correct]**
2. two acute angles, one obtuse angle, no equal sides, scalene **[2 marks for all correct and no incorrect statements ticked, 1 mark for at least two correct]**
3. a) acute scalene
   b) right-angled isosceles

Challenge 3
1. 45°
2. a)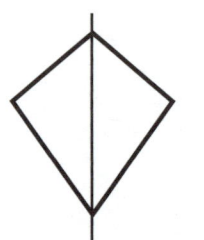

   b)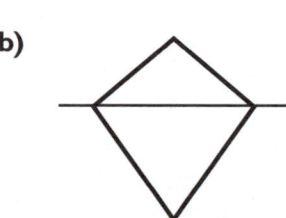

Pages 92–93

Challenge 1
1. a) cone
   b) cylinder
   c) square-based pyramid
   d) triangular prism

Challenge 2
1. a) cube   b) square
2. a) 30 cm b) 9 cm
3. sphere

Challenge 3
1. 14
2. sphere and cylinder (or upside-down cone)
3. a) cuboid   b) 6 cm
4. a) square-based pyramid
   b) triangle-based pyramid
   c) triangular prism

Pages 94–95

Challenge 1

1. a)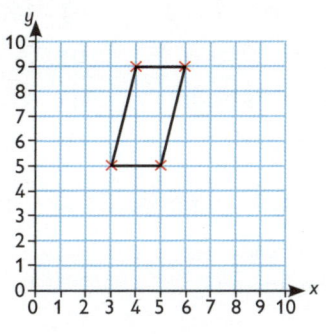

   [2 marks for all points correct, 1 mark if one incorrect]

   b) parallelogram

Challenge 2

1. a)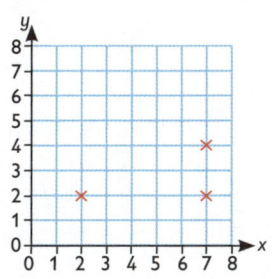

   b) (2, 4)
2. (4, 5)
3. a) (2, 4)
   b) $(5\frac{1}{2}, 3)$

Challenge 3

1. a) (5, 6)   b) (7, 4)
2. a) 12 cm   b) 8 cm^2
3. (4, 5)
4. Any two from: (5, 0), (1, 4) and (7, 8)

Pages 96–97

Challenge 1

1. 6
2. 5, down

Challenge 2

1. 3 squares right, 3 squares down
2.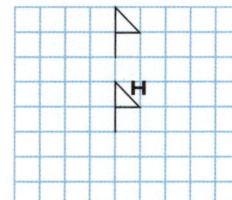
3. a)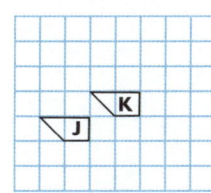

   b) 2 squares right, 1 square up

Challenge 3

1.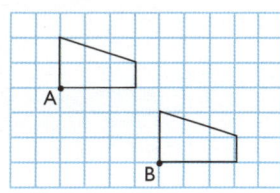
2. 4 squares left, 3 squares up
3.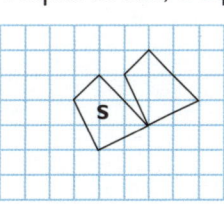

Pages 98–99

Challenge 1

1. C
2.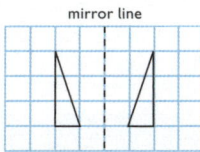
3.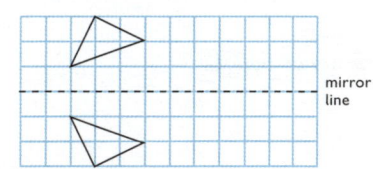

Challenge 2

1.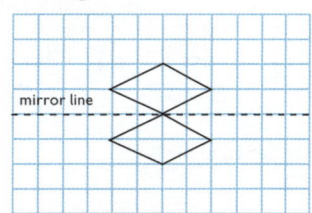
2.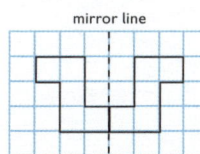
3.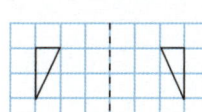
4.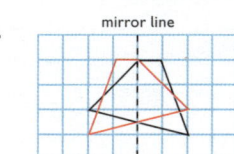

Challenge 3

1.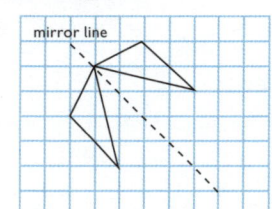

2.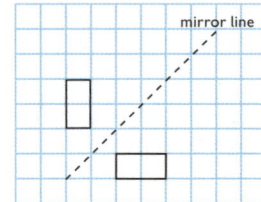

3. a)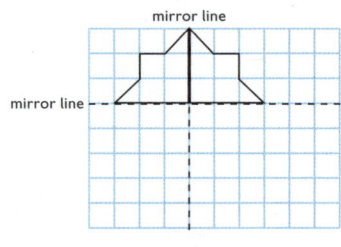

   b)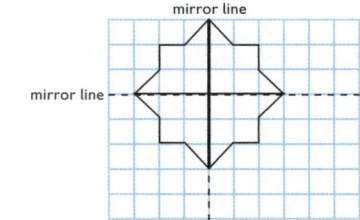

   c) 4

Pages 100–101
Challenge 1
1.
Shape	Number of shapes
Triangle	3
Quadrilateral	6
Pentagon	2

2. a) 10 b) 20 c) 46 d) yellow

Challenge 2
1. a) Class 3 b) 9 c) Class 4 d) Class 5
2. a) and b)

Time interval	Number of birds
9.00 to 9.05 am	IIII
11.00 to 11.05 am	ℍ I
1.00 to 1.05 pm	ℍ ℍ
3.00 to 3.05 pm	ℍ III
4.00 to 4.05 pm	III

c) 1.00 to 1.05 pm

Challenge 3
1. Guinea pig 2, Parrot 2, Rabbit 4
2. a) 13 b) Monday c) Athletics

Pages 102–103
Challenge 1
1. a) Marseille b) 4 minutes
   c) Marseille d) 10 hours 28 minutes

Challenge 2
1. a) 08:28 b) 33 minutes
   c) 17 minutes d) 07:55

Challenge 3
1. a) Train 2 b) 24 minutes
   c) Train 2 d) 15:42 e) 16:59
2. a) Maths b) 3
   c) 30 minutes or ½ hour d) 1¼ hours
   e) Maths and English f) 5¼ hours

Pages 104–105
Challenge 1
1.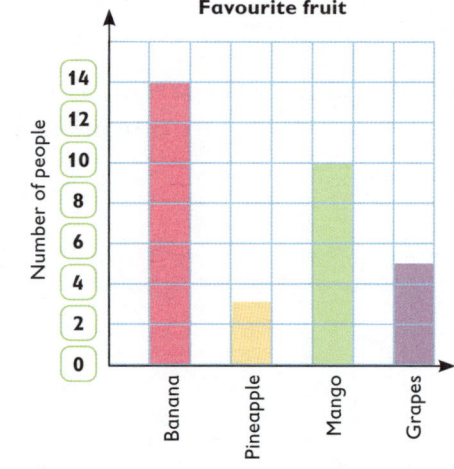

2. a) 13
   b)
   Sandwiches sold

Mon	⊠ ⊠ ⊠ ⊠
Tues	⊠ ⊠ ⊠ ⊠ ▽
Weds	⊠ ⊠ ⊠ ▽
Thurs	⊠ ⊠ ⊠ ⊠ ▽
Fri	⊠ ⊠ ▽

   Key ⊠ = 4 sandwiches

Challenge 2
1. a) 40 b) 80 c) 95

Challenge 3
1. a) Roller Coaster b) Heights
   c) Relaxing River d) 110

Pages 106–107
Challenge 1
1.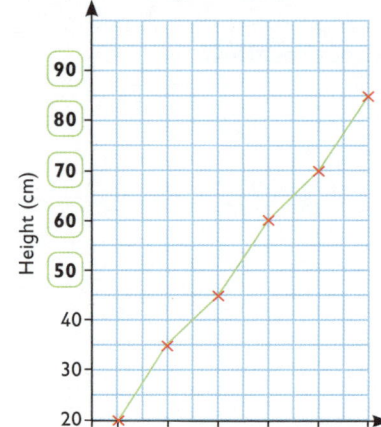

Challenge 2
1. a) Sunday   b) 60   c) 10   d) 4

Challenge 3
1. a) 1 pm and 3 pm   b) 9 am and 1 pm
   c) 3 pm and 5 pm   d) 0°C
   e) 4 hours
2. a) 7.5 seconds
   b) 5.5 metres
   c) 2 seconds and 6.5 seconds

Progress test 4
Pages 108–112

1. Angle between 90° and 180°, e.g.

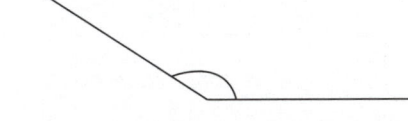

2. Accurate 30° angle, drawn using a protractor
3. 1580
4. a) any one of A, C, D, E, F, G
   b) F   c) B   d) C, D   e) E
5. 8°C
6. 18 cm³
7. a) 12   b) $4\frac{1}{2}$
8. 30°
9. a) 46 m   b) 126 m²
10. a, d and f   [2 marks if all correct, 1 mark if one incorrect]
11. right-angled scalene
12. 190°
13. a)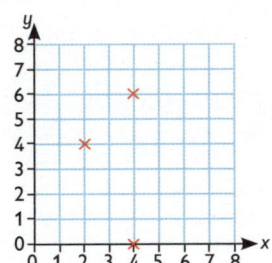

    b) (6, 4)
14. 10%   0.25 $\frac{3}{5}$ 75%   0.8
    [2 marks if all correct, 1 mark if one incorrect]
15. 14:06
16. 45°
17. a) Thursday   b) 12   c) 7

Notes

Progress test charts

Use these charts to record your results in the four Progress tests. Colour in the questions that you got right to help you identify any areas that you might need to study and practise again. (These areas are indicated in the 'See page…' row in the charts.)

Progress test 1:

	Q1	Q2	Q3	Q4	Q5	Q6	Q7	Q8	Q9	Q10	Q11	Q12	Q13	Q14	Q15	Q16
See page…	12-13	12-13	20-21	28-29	16-17	12-13	20-21	12-13	24-25	18-19	26-27	30-31	12-13	22-23	14-15	26-27

	Q17	Q18	Q19	Q20	Q21	Q22	Q23	Q24	Q25	Q26	Q27	Q28	Q29	Q30	Q31	TOTAL /48
See page…	18-19	28-29	16-17	30-31	14-15	20-21	24-25	14-15	28-29	24-25	16-17	20-21	20-21	20-21	22-23	

Progress test 2:

	Q1	Q2	Q3	Q4	Q5	Q6	Q7	Q8	Q9	Q10	Q11	Q12
See page…	24-25	36-37	20-21	18-19	44-45	52-53	14-15	42-43	18-19	52-53	20-21	46-47

	Q13	Q14	Q15	Q16	Q17	Q18	Q19	Q20	Q21	Q22	Q23	Q24
See page…	38-39	48-49	12-13	42-43	36-37	46-47	38-39	46-47	16-17	48-49	20-21	40-41

	Q25	Q26	Q27	Q28	Q29	Q30	Q31	Q32	Q33	Q34	Q35	Q36	TOTAL /60
See page…	26-27	46-47	44-45	28-29	46-47	28-29	50-51	38-39	44-45	52-53	22-23	12-13	

Progress test 3:

	Q1	Q2	Q3	Q4	Q5	Q6	Q7	Q8	Q9	Q10	Q11	Q12	Q13	Q14	Q15
See page…	50-51	26-27	64-65	16-17	64-65	58-59	66-67	48-49	58-59	60-63	38-39	50-51	18-19	64-65	58-59

	Q16	Q17	Q18	Q19	Q20	Q21	Q22	Q23	Q24	Q25	Q26	Q27	Q28	Q29	TOTAL /38
See page…	66-67	20-21	74-75	64-65	30-31	38-39	20-21	66-67	42-43	64-65	64-65	64-65	74-75	74-75	

Progress test 4:

	Q1	Q2	Q3	Q4	Q5	Q6	Q7	Q8	Q9	Q10	Q11	Q12	Q13	Q14	Q15	Q16	Q17	TOTAL /30
See page…	80-81	82-83	16-17	84-85	18-19	68-69	52-53	82-83	60-63	84-85	90-91	82-83	94-95	50-51	102-103	82-83	106-107	

What am I doing well in?

....

....

....

What do I need to improve?

....

....

....